MARY BERRY'S

CHRISTMAS COLLECTION

*Over 100 of my fabulous recipes and
tips for a hassle-free festive season*

headline

OTHER BOOKS BY MARY BERRY INCLUDE:

Mary Berry's Family Sunday Lunches
Cook Now, Eat Later
Mary Berry's Stress-free Kitchen
Real Food – Fast
Mary Berry's New Aga Cookbook

This edition first published in 2013
by HEADLINE BOOK PUBLISHING

Some of the recipes in this book have
previously appeared in *Mary Berry's New
Aga Cookbook*, *Cook Now, Eat Later* and
Real Food – Fast. *Mary Berry's Christmas
Collection* was first published in 2006.

10 9 8 7 6 5 4 3

Cataloguing in Publication Data
is available from the British Library.
978 0 7553 6441 1

Edited by Jo Roberts-Miller
Designed by Smith & Gilmour
Photography by Martin Poole
Food Stylist: Kim Morphew
Assistant Food Stylist: Poppy Campbell
Prop Stylist: Lydia Brun
Printed and bound in Germany by Mohn Media

Headline's policy is to use papers that are
natural, renewable and recyclable products
and made from wood grown in sustainable
forests. The logging and manufacturing
processes are expected to conform to the
environmental regulations of the country
of origin.

HEADLINE BOOK PUBLISHING
An Hachette UK Company
338 Euston Road
London NW1 3BH

www.headline.co.uk
www.hachette.co.uk

CONTENTS

INTRODUCTION

Christmas to me is a time for celebration, for family, for laughter and good food. I remember the times when I used to prepare everything at home – the turkey, vegetables, stuffing, Christmas pudding – and take it to Granny's on Christmas Eve, ready to be cooked the next day. Children, gifts, crackers, dogs, cats – everything had to be remembered and organised meticulously. Although these days most of my Christmases are at home, and the young come back to us with their children, the advance preparation and organisation doesn't seem to be getting much less.

For, however many times you have done it before, it does still seem very daunting, especially when, as far as the high-street shops are concerned, Christmas is upon us as soon as the summer holidays are over! That is why I thought it might be a good idea to gather together my recipes, my ideas and my snippets of wisdom – all gained over the years – into this guide to happy, care-free Christmas cooking.

The first edition of this book was published seven years ago – since then cooking has changed in some ways: there are new techniques and ingredients so we've added some new recipes, and retested or tweaked the other ones. We've photographed nearly every single recipe this time, too – there's nothing more inviting and helpful than seeing the finished dish to aim for.

The recipes themselves are on the whole traditional, but you will find many of them have a modern twist, which gives them that special touch. Often I will add an unexpected new flavouring ingredient, for we are always experimenting with flavours. However, the best flavour comes from the best ingredients which is what you start with. I never cut corners in terms of ingredients and I would always encourage everyone to use the very best available. I buy fresh meat, fresh fish and vegetables from local shops, farmers' markets and so on, but I am also very much in favour of many of the ready-prepared ingredients you can find these days in good delicatessens and supermarkets – things such as jars of roasted peppers, tubs of crème fraîche or hummus, cans of chickpeas or cannellini beans. Most of these are very good indeed, and save you so much time. If you had some of those in your storecupboard or larder, you would always have the basis for a quick meal during the holiday period, and you wouldn't have to panic about running or driving to the nearest, probably closed, shops!

Most of my books over the years have contained notes about preparing and freezing in advance – perhaps the most important aspect for the cook at Christmas – and this one is no exception. You will find many hints and tips which will help you to plan and organise your Christmas without stress – not least the Christmas menus, Christmas countdown and virtually a minute-by-minute review of cooking the Christmas lunch, which follow this introduction. (This took us *ages* to do, and we do hope it will be useful.) My previous books have usually contained information for those among you who are Aga fans, and you have not been ignored here. I actually couldn't write a recipe without thinking about how it would cook in the Aga, for I have been using one for more years than I care to remember. It's like one of my oldest friends.

We all wish you very happy cooking, a Merry Christmas, and a Happy New Year.

Mary Berry

CHRISTMAS LUNCH MENUS

Here are a few menu ideas for you to chose from. If you decide not to have a first course, serve small open brown-bread sandwiches topped with smoked salmon or gravadlax with drinks before lunch.
To follow, I always serve two puds.

MENU ONE
TRADITIONAL ROAST TURKEY

Smoked Salmon or Gravadlax
with Mustard Dill Sauce
brown bread and butter

Traditional Roast Turkey
Lemon and Thyme
Pork Stuffing
Apricot and Chestnut
Stuffing
Bread Sauce
Scarlet Confit
Christmas Turkey Gravy
For vegetarian guests
Aubergine Five-nut Roast
with Italian Tomato Sauce

Roast Potatoes
Roast Parsnips
Buttered Brussels Sprouts
Braised Red Cabbage
Celeriac Purée
Sausages Wrapped in Bacon

Christmas Pudding
Brandy Butter, Boozy Cream,
Brandy Sauce or
Brandy Ice Cream
Classic Old-fashioned Trifle

Coffee and Chocolate

MENU TWO
ROAST BEEF

Fresh Salmon and
Dill Terrines
brown bread and butter

Prime Rib of Beef and Gravy
Yorkshire Pudding
For vegetarian guests
Aubergine and Goat's
Cheese Roast

Roast Potatoes
Roast Parsnips
Celeriac Purée
Braised Red Cabbage
Beetroot and Horseradish

Frangipane Mince Pies
Brandy Butter, Boozy Cream,
Brandy Sauce or
Brandy Ice Cream
Chocolate Log

Coffee and Chocolate

MENU THREE
ROAST GOOSE

Carlton Pâté
toast

Roast Goose and Gravy
Sage and Onion Stuffing
Apple Sauce
For vegetarian guests
Char-grilled Vegetable
Strudel with Roquefort

Roast Squash and
Sweet Potato
Parisienne Potatoes
Buttered Brussels Sprouts

Christmas Tarte Amandine
Chocolate Roulade

Coffee and Chocolate

CHRISTMAS LUNCH SHOPPING LIST

Below is a shopping list to end all shopping lists, including everything you will need for my suggested Roast Turkey Christmas lunch.

STORECUPBOARD STAPLES

flour (plain and self-raising)
sugar (caster, granulated
  and light muscovado)
salt (cooking and sea salt)
pepper, black
oil (olive and sunflower)
mustard, Dijon
spices (allspice, cinnamon,
  nutmeg, cloves)
herbs (dried dill, bay leaves)
vinegar (white wine, cider)
sun-dried tomato paste
Worcestershire sauce
apricot jam/strawberry jam/
  redcurrant jelly
almond extract
glycerine
dried dates

STORECUPBOARD
INGREDIENTS TO BUY IN

2 × 500g cartons tomato passata
225g (8 oz) dried apricots
1 × 400g (14 oz) can pears
  in natural juice
1 packet trifle sponges,
  containing 8 sponges
about 10 ratafia biscuits
350g (12 oz) frozen chestnuts
25g (1 oz) flaked almonds
175g (6 oz) mixed nuts
50g (2 oz) pistachio nuts
225g (8 oz) ground almonds
truffles or chocolates to
  serve with coffee

MEAT

6.3kg (14 lb) fresh oven-ready
  turkey, plus giblets
675g (1½ lb) pork
  sausagemeat
6 slices good streaky bacon
18 cocktail sausages

FISH

1.8kg (4 lb) whole fresh
  salmon, for gravadlax,
  filleted to give two sides of
  salmon, or 500g (1 lb 2 oz)
  slices smoked salmon

DAIRY

10 large eggs
750g (1 lb 10 oz) butter
100g (4 oz) unsalted butter
jar of goose fat
1 × 200ml (7 fl oz) carton
  full-fat crème fraîche
450ml (¾ pint) milk
450ml (¾ pint) double cream
600ml (1 pint) good-quality
  fresh vanilla custard
100g (4 oz) mature
  Cheddar cheese

FRUIT AND VEGETABLES

a bunch of fresh dill
fresh thyme sprigs
2 generous bunches
  of fresh parsley
6 lemons
7 onions
3 celery sticks
1 large carrot
1 bulb garlic
1.4kg (3 lb) old potatoes,
  such as Désirée, King
  Edward, Maris Piper
900g (2 lb) parsnips
900g (2 lb) Brussels sprouts
1 large red cabbage, about
  1kg (2¼ lb)
450g (1 lb) cooking apples
1.8kg (4 lb) celeriac
450g (1 lb) fresh or frozen
  cranberries
1 orange
1 medium aubergine

BAKERY

2 large white tin loaves
  for breadcrumbs
brown bread to serve
  with smoked salmon
  or gravadlax

ALCOHOL

port
red and white wines
brandy or Cognac
medium dry sherry
champagne
non-alchoholic drinks

COUNTDOWN TO CHRISTMAS

What follows is a countdown for the Traditional Roast Turkey Menu – it's what we do at home.

IN THE FREEZER

It is always a good feeling to have started Christmas preparations early. The following dishes can be frozen up to 3 weeks ahead for Christmas lunch:

Gravadlax

Bread Sauce

Scarlet Confit

Apricot and Chestnut Stuffing

Sausages Wrapped in Bacon

Braised Red Cabbage

Aubergine Five-nut Roast and Italian Tomato Sauce

Christmas Pudding

Brandy Butter

MORE THAN A WEEK BEFORE

* Make the Christmas pudding and Christmas cake up to 8 weeks ahead.

* Shop for storecupboard ingredients and booze. It is always worth having extra eggs, olive and sunflower oil, lemons, etc.

* Reorganise the fridge so that you have room for all of the perishable foods. Make more room by taking out anything that will be fine kept at a cool temperature, such as vegetables… and keep these in the garage or a cool place instead.

A WEEK BEFORE

* Make the brandy butter, spoon into a serving dish, cover and keep in the fridge.

* Almond paste and ice the Christmas cake.

ON 23 DECEMBER

* Do any last-minute perishable shopping.

* To get ahead and to make sure that you feel fully in control on Christmas Day, the following dishes can be made, cooled where appropriate, and kept in the fridge, if not already prepared and frozen:

Prepare the Lemon and Thyme Stuffing.

Make the Giblet Stock, cool and strain.

Prepare the Sausages Wrapped in Bacon.

Braise the Red Cabbage.

Make the Scarlet Confit.

Prepare the Apricot and Chestnut Stuffing today, cook on 24th and reheat on Christmas Day.

Prepare the Gravadlax and mustard dill sauce.

Cook the Aubergine Five-nut Roast and its Italian Tomato Sauce.

* Peel the potatoes and keep in water.

* Take butter out of the fridge to soften for turkey.

ON 24 DECEMBER

✳ Take frozen foods out of the freezer and leave in a cool place overnight to thaw, or meat or fish dishes to thaw in the fridge.

✳ I always parboil and half roast the potatoes and parsnips the day before so that they simply need a quick blast in the oven to re-roast on Christmas day. Make sure that you don't use too much fat or the potatoes may well become soggy. Drain excess fat once half roasted.

✳ Brussels sprouts can be trimmed of their outer discoloured leaves and kept in a polythene bag in the fridge – they should not be kept in water.

✳ Cook the Apricot and Chestnut Stuffing, cool and keep in the fridge ready to reheat.

✳ Make the Celeriac Purée, cool, then spoon into a buttered ovenproof dish ready to reheat.

✳ Make the Classic Old-fashioned Trifle but don't decorate with toasted flaked almonds just yet as they will lose their crunch!

✳ Stuff the turkey and calculate cooking time (see page 101).

✳ Make the Gravy with the Giblet Stock, making it slightly thicker than you want it as you will be adding the skimmed roasting juices from the cooked turkey on Christmas Day.

✳ Infuse and strain milk for the Bread Sauce, if not frozen.

✳ Take the Gravadlax out of the curing juices. Wrap and freeze half of it for another time and wrap the other half and keep in the fridge ready for slicing.

✳ Lay the table, sort out serving dishes and plates.

✳ Chill white wine and champagne (if you are spoiling everyone).

CHRISTMAS DAY (TO SERVE AT 2PM)

The timings I have given for Christmas lunch are based on a 6.3kg (14 lb) turkey, using an ordinary domestic double oven.

7.40AM Take turkey out of fridge to bring to come to room temperature before cooking. Arrange oven shelves so that the turkey will fit.

8.10AM Preheat the oven to 220°C/Fan 200°C/Gas 7 and cover the turkey in foil.

8.40AM Turkey into oven for 40 minutes at the high temperature.

9.20AM Reduce oven temperature to 160°C/Fan 140°C/Gas 3 and cook turkey for a further 3½ hours, basting now and again.

10.00AM Arrange smoked salmon or gravadlax on plates for first course. Butter brown bread. Cover the plates with clingfilm and keep in the fridge.

12.30PM Re-steam Christmas pudding to reheat. Warm plates and serving dishes if you have a hot plate. If using a second oven, heat in a low oven later.

1.00PM Check to see if the turkey is nearly cooked – turn back foil and turn heat up to 220°C/Fan 200ºC/ Gas 7 for last 30 minutes to crisp skin. Put sausages wrapped in bacon into the second oven, at 190°C/ Fan 170ºC/ Gas 5 for 45 minutes until cooked and crisp.

1.20PM Reheat aubergine five-nut roast, if serving, at 190°C/Fan 170ºC/ Gas 5 for about 30 minutes. Take turkey out of oven. Test to make sure it is cooked. Leave to relax, loosely covered in foil and a thick towel for about 30 minutes before carving. Re-roast potatoes (half roasted) in oven at 220°C/Fan 200ºC/ Gas 7. Reheat celeriac purée (covered in foil) and apricot stuffing in the second oven for 30 minutes. Reheat red cabbage on hob in a large pan, or microwave for a few minutes, spoon into a serving dish and keep warm. Arrange first courses on the table.

1.40PM Re-roast parsnips (half roasted) by putting into the same hot oven with the potatoes. Reheat gravy, adding skimmed roasting juices from the cooked turkey. Check seasoning. Gently reheat scarlet confit in a pan on the hob, spoon into a serving dish and keep warm. Heat serving dishes and plates (if you didn't do so before).

1.50PM Cook sprouts, drain and put in serving dish. Carve the turkey. Add a little milk and reheat the bread sauce gently in a small pan on the hob. Reheat tomato sauce to go with the aubergine five-nut roast, if serving, in a medium pan on the hob. Remove everything from the ovens, and put into warm serving dishes.

2.00PM Check water level on Christmas pudding, before you sit down to eat. Serve lunch.

LATER ... Serve Christmas pudding with brandy butter or chosen sauce. Scatter toasted flaked almonds on to trifle.

TIPS FOR A
STRESS-FREE CHRISTMAS

Christmas lunch really is one meal where it is well worth doing as much preparation and cooking in advance as you can so that you have as little to do as possible at the last minute. Even if you've cooked Christmas lunch many times before, it is always a challenge. Here are some tips to make it all as stress-free as possible. One of the biggest tasks at Christmas is the shopping. Buy all of the larder or storecupboard ingredients and booze well ahead, and store where they will not get used by mistake before the big day!

SHOPPING AHEAD

Perishable items can all be bought by 23 December; there shouldn't be any need to rush to the shops on Christmas Eve. Remember that most supermarkets are open long hours in the run-up to Christmas and some also deliver. If you are really pushed you can order your groceries online.

TALKING TURKEYS

Order a fresh turkey in good time from your butcher or supermarket, or even online from a specialist supplier. It is worth asking in advance how much notice they need. Also ask whether they deliver – one less thing for you to do!

If you are ordering a larger turkey than you usually cook, do check that it will fit in the oven!

Fresh turkeys are best, but if you do buy a frozen bird take care to thaw it thoroughly. Thaw the turkey in a cool place such as the garage, not in the fridge or in water. Watch the temperature outside though, because if it is freezing the turkey will take longer to thaw. Aim to have the turkey defrosted completely and into the fridge by Christmas Eve. When thawed the meat should be soft and the cavity ice free. Check that the legs move freely from the breast too.

Remove the giblets from a fresh bird at once, and as soon as they are loose from a frozen bird, cover and keep in the fridge or use straightaway to make giblet stock.

Allow the turkey to come to room temperature for about 1 hour before cooking.

Time the turkey so that it has at least half an hour to rest before carving.

IS THE TURKEY COOKED?

Remember that ovens vary and although you can work out the approximate time to cook your turkey (see the chart on page 101), it is still essential to test it with a meat thermometer or by using a skewer. Insert the dial/spike type of thermometer into the thickest part of the turkey thigh at the beginning of cooking. The digital type of meat thermometer goes into the turkey to test the temperature at the end (see also page 99).

To test whether the turkey is cooked with a skewer, insert the skewer into the thickest part of the thigh and check the juices – they should run clear when the turkey is cooked. If the juices are still pink, then the turkey is not yet cooked. Pull the legs away from the breast to allow the heat to circulate and return the turkey to the oven for about 15–30 minutes before testing again. Cover the breast of the turkey with foil to protect it from getting too dark and drying out.

RESTING THE TURKEY

Loosely cover the whole cooked turkey with foil, then also with clean towels to keep the heat in. The turkey will happily sit like this for up to 2 hours and still be piping hot when carved.

While the turkey is resting there is plenty of time to cook the sausages wrapped in bacon, re-roast the potatoes and parsnips, and reheat the vegetables, stuffing, bread sauce, scarlet confit and gravy.

If you get terribly behind with the remaining preparations (or the family are delayed), then simply put the turkey back into the oven at a high temperature at the last minute.

Any leftover turkey needs to be cooled and put into the fridge as soon as possible – don't leave it hanging around in a hot steamy kitchen!

CARVING THE TURKEY

I find it easier to carve one side of the turkey first. Take off one leg and cut in half to give a drumstick and thigh. Carve the meat from the leg – you may find this easier with a smaller knife – and slice the thigh meat. Cut the wing off the bird as close to the breast as possible, then slice the breast meat on the diagonal, including some stuffing. Arrange the meats and sliced stuffing on a serving platter so everyone can have a little light meat from the breast and dark meat from the legs.

GRAVY ISSUES

Lumpy gravy? Simply sieve or you could use a hand-held blender to destroy the lumps.

If your gravy is too thin, add a teaspoon of cornflour mixed with a little cold water or stock, then bring back to the boil to thicken.

Adding the skimmed juices from the roasted turkey enhances the flavour of the gravy no end, but if yours still seems a little tasteless, check seasoning and then add a dash of Worcestershire sauce.

A FEW REMINDERS

Sharpen knives well ahead.

Make sure you have supplies of extra-wide foil, kitchen roll, clingfilm and non-stick baking paper. It is good to have a large spoon for basting. A skewer or meat thermometer is essential for testing the turkey.

If oven space is short, then half-roast the parsnips and potatoes the day before (see pages 130 and 131).

If your Christmas pudding is traditional, and contains a high proportion of sugar, dried fruits, fat and alcohol, it can be reheated in the microwave. All these ingredients quickly reach a high temperature in the microwave. It is a good idea to be on hand while the pudding reheats, and reheat for slightly less time than directed to begin with. Also check the power of your microwave and refer to the manufacturer's handbook if in doubt.

Remove the foil and paper from the pudding and microwave on 750W for about 3 minutes. If not cooked, cook again at 1-minute intervals. Leave to stand for 2 minutes before serving.

CANAPÉS

CHAPTER ONE

In most of my books there are hints and tips about preparing in advance, and at no time is this more important than when making canapés, or nibbles to go with drinks. This could be on Christmas Eve, pre Boxing Day lunch, or at New Year some time. Because they are so small, canapés can be very time-consuming, especially when you are preparing them for a crowd. Thinking about it all well in advance is a good idea, particularly at Christmas, when you have so many other meals to consider.

You can of course offer many nibbles that can be bought, and need no preparation at all, just decanting into a bowl. I'm thinking about things such as good stoneless or stuffed olives, or potato or vegetable crisps. But it's nice to offer something homemade. The croûtons on page 28, for instance, are delicious and can be baked straight from the freezer. The biscuits on page 18 can also be made in advance, then simply crisped up momentarily in a hot oven. The Jumbo Prawns in Teriyaki Sauce on page 26, meanwhile, can be marinated ahead of time and are ready to cook in no time at all. Dips are always useful, too, and take moments to prepare a little in advance; all you need is a selection of pretty bowls to put them in, and something to dip – crudités of raw veg (which have to be cut at the last minute, I must admit), or crispbreads or breadsticks. You could always offer boiled quail's eggs with drinks: pile them in a bowl, some of them peeled, some not – this looks very attractive – and serve with celery salt.

The important thing is to consider what it is you are offering – and make it clear to your guests as well! As it is pre lunch or dinner, you are not giving them a meal, just something to accompany drinks. Bite-sized canapés are the order of the day usually, and I work on about five per person. At a pinch, you could make this slightly more substantial, viewing your canapés as the starter to the meal. Then you can go straight to the main course when sitting down at table.

SMOKED SALMON CANAPÉS

Rye bread, usually from Denmark or Germany, is available already sliced in packets, sometimes with sunflower seeds added. Of course you could use ordinary brown bread or blinis, but rye bread is more unusual and much more practical. The texture of the bread means that it holds up well, not going soggy once the topping is added, and so these are ideal to be made ahead.

6 slices rye bread
1 × 200g (7 oz) packet full-fat
   cream cheese
2 × 125g (4½ oz) packets
   smoked salmon (minimum
   3 slices in each)
freshly ground black pepper
a little freshly squeezed
   lemon juice (optional)

TO GARNISH
sprigs of fresh dill
black lumpfish caviar

STEP 1 Spread the bread generously with the cream cheese. Cut each slice of bread into eight equal squares.

STEP 2 Cut the smoked salmon into 48 small pieces.

STEP 3 Top each square with smoked salmon, piling the salmon on generously so that it doesn't lie flat. Season with freshly ground black pepper and a squeeze of lemon juice if wished.

STEP 4 Garnish each with a small sprig of fresh dill or a little black lumpfish caviar. Arrange on a serving platter.

PREPARING AHEAD The rye bread holds up so well that these can be made the day before. Cover the canapés tightly with clingfilm and keep in the fridge.

TIP If you don't like rye bread, use an interesting brown loaf cut fairly thinly instead. You could also pipe the cream cheese on to the squares of bread.

PARMESAN AND PISTACHIO NUTTERS

V

A wonderful biscuit, for nibbles with a glass of wine before dinner.
Do be careful not to overcook them, as they burn very easily!

100g (4 oz) butter, very soft
50g (2 oz) semolina
85g (3½ oz) self-raising flour
75g (3 oz) Parmesan, grated
a good pinch of dry
  mustard powder
salt and freshly ground
  black pepper
40 small pistachio nuts, shelled

Preheat the oven to 180ºC/Fan 160ºC/Gas 4.

STEP 1 Measure all the ingredients, except the nuts, into a large bowl and work together until combined to a soft dough. This can also be done in a food processor.

STEP 2 Roll the dough into about 40 small balls. Arrange on a large baking sheet and press so they resemble a very thick £2 coin. Press a nut into the centre of each.

STEP 3 Bake in the preheated oven for 15–20 minutes until pale golden brown – you will need to keep an eye on them! Cool on a wire rack and serve cold.

AGA Bake on the grid shelf on the floor of the Roasting Oven, with the cold plain shelf on the second set of runners for 12–15 minutes until golden brown.

PREPARING AHEAD These freeze brilliantly cooked: just defrost and refresh in a medium oven to crisp them up before serving. They can also be made up to a week ahead and kept in an airtight container lined with kitchen paper.

TIP You can use other nuts to top the biscuits. I have an aversion to peanuts, but you could use them, or why not try cashews or pine nuts instead of the pistachios? You can also use 2 teaspoons to spoon out blobs – these will not be perfectly shaped but at least they look homemade!

ROQUEFORT AND PEAR CROSTINI

V

Unusual and delicious for a small drinks party; too time-consuming to do for 100! These must be served warm. They even reheat well once made, but they look their best straight from the oven.

1 × 400g (14 oz) can pears, in natural juice
100g (4 oz) Roquefort cheese
paprika
chopped fresh chives

CROSTINI
1 small, thin baguette
olive oil
salt and freshly ground black pepper

Preheat the grill to its highest setting.

STEP 1 First make the crostini. Thinly slice the baguette, brush both sides with oil, season and place on a small baking sheet which will fit under the grill or in the grill pan lined with foil.

STEP 2 To cook the crostini, toast under the grill for 2–3 minutes each side until pale golden brown and crisp. Watch them carefully. Cool on a wire rack.

STEP 3 Drain and cut the pears into small cubes about the size of a raisin.

STEP 4 The next process is messy! Coarsely grate the cheese into a bowl. Stir in the pear cubes and spread the mixture on to the crostini.

STEP 5 When ready to serve, sprinkle with paprika and place under a hot grill for 4–5 minutes or until the cheese has melted. Sprinkle with chives.

AGA For the crostini, arrange them on a baking sheet, and cook on the floor of the Roasting Oven, turning once, until golden brown, about 5 minutes. To cook when assembled, slide the baking sheet on to the second set of runners in the Roasting Oven for 4–5 minutes until pale golden and the cheese has melted on the crostini. Watch very carefully. Allow to cool for a moment, then scatter with chives and serve.

PREPARING AHEAD These can be assembled up to 12 hours ahead. Cover with clingfilm and keep in the fridge until needed. Grill to serve.

TIP The crostini can be made up to 2 months in advance and frozen. Defrost and assemble with the pears and Roquefort.

⚜ DIPS IN MINUTES ⚜

V

RED PEPPER AND HERB
Measure 2 canned red peppers, drained, 2 roughly chopped spring onions, a small bunch of fresh basil, and a few sprigs each of fresh parsley and dill in a processor and whiz. Add 8 tablespoons lowcalorie mayonnaise and process again. Season with salt and pepper, put into a serving bowl, cover with clingfilm and chill. Can be made up to 3 days ahead and kept in the fridge.

SPICED MANGO
Combine 225g (8 oz) half-fat cream cheese with 1 tablespoon curry powder, 4 tablespoons mango chutney and the juice of ½ lemon. Season with salt and pepper, put into a serving bowl, cover with clingfilm and chill. Can be made up to 3 days ahead and kept in the fridge.

GUACAMOLE
Peel a large ripe avocado, and cut the flesh into chunks. Coarsely chop 4 spring onions. Peel and deseed 2 large firm tomatoes, put them into the processor with the other ingredients and whiz until smooth. Stir in a dash each of Tabasco, sugar and lemon juice, plus some salt and pepper to taste, and whiz again. Put into a serving bowl, cover with clingfilm and chill. Make on the day of serving.

BLUE CHEESE
Measure 100g (4 oz) Dolcelatte or Stilton cheese into the processor, add a 150ml carton soured cream and a little pepper and whiz. Put into a serving bowl, cover with clingfilm and chill. Can be made up to 3 days ahead and kept in the fridge.

MILD CHILLI
Mix a 200ml (7 fl oz) carton of low-fat crème fraîche with 4 tablespoons bought chilli dipping sauce, stir well, and season with salt and pepper. Perfect with prawns or chicken goujons. Put into a serving bowl, cover with clingfilm and chill. Can be made up to 3 days ahead and kept in the fridge.

GOOD THINGS FOR DIPPING

RAW VEGETABLES
Pencil thickness and about 7.5cm (3 in) long sticks of carrot, red or yellow pepper, courgette, cucumber or celery. Halved baby sweetcorn and tiny mangetout or sugar-snap peas are ideal too.

GARLIC PITTA BREAD
Melt 50g (2 oz) butter and mix with 2 crushed garlic cloves. Brush this over the cut side of 4 large pitta breads, split in half horizontally. Arrange on a foil-lined grill pan and sprinkle with salt and pepper. Slide under the grill and cook for about 5 minutes until golden brown and crispy. Slice into triangles and serve. To cook in the Aga, arrange on a baking sheet and slide on to the top set of runners in the Roasting Oven for about 6 minutes until golden brown.

BREADSTICKS
These are ideal for dipping – but a little boring!

QUAIL'S EGG AND HOLLANDAISE MINI TARTLETS

It is very time-consuming making tiny pastry cases, but you can buy some very good ones in supermarkets and delicatessens.

24 mini cocktail pastry cases

FILLING
12 quail's eggs
24 small asparagus tips
salt and freshly ground
    black pepper
a little bought olive tapenade
a little bought good
    hollandaise sauce
paprika
a little melted butter

Preheat the oven to 150°C/Fan 130°C/Gas 2.

STEP 1 Boil the eggs in boiling water for about 2 minutes (this will give a soft yolk), drain and refresh in cold water. Peel at once, carefully, as they are soft-boiled.

STEP 2 Blanch the asparagus tips in boiling salted water until just tender. Refresh in cold water, and dry using kitchen paper.

STEP 3 Spoon a little olive tapenade into the base of each pastry case.

STEP 4 Carefully slice each quail's egg in half lengthways and put one half in the base of each case. Season, spoon over a little hollandaise sauce and sprinkle with paprika. Top with the asparagus tips and brush with a little melted butter.

STEP 5 Arrange on a small baking sheet and heat through in the preheated oven for about 12 minutes until warm. Serve warm.

AGA Heat on a baking sheet in the Simmering Oven for about 10 minutes.

PREPARING AHEAD They can be prepared about 6 hours ahead, but not longer than that, or they could become soggy.

TIP If preferred, you can replace the olive tapenade with sun-dried tomato paste or pesto.

JUMBO PRAWNS IN TERIYAKI SAUCE

Peeled jumbo prawns are available in the freezer department in supermarkets; thaw to use.

30 raw jumbo prawns, peeled
salt and freshly ground
   black pepper
a knob of butter
30 small wooden
   cocktail skewers

TERIYAKI SAUCE
6 tablespoons brown sauce
3 tablespoons soy sauce
6 tablespoons water
½ teaspoon white wine vinegar
½ teaspoon ginger, finely grated
2 level teaspoons cornflour

STEP 1 Put the prawns into a bowl and season.

STEP 2 Measure all of the sauce ingredients into a small saucepan. Whisk until smooth then heat on the hob, stirring, until the sauce has thickened. Pour into a bowl and leave to become completely cold.

STEP 3 Pour half of the cold sauce over the prawns. Set aside the remaining sauce for dipping.

STEP 4 Heat the butter in a frying pan. Fry the prawns over a high heat until lightly golden, pink inside and cooked through.

STEP 5 Thread each prawn on to a skewer or cocktail stick and serve on a platter with the dipping sauce

AGA Cook in a frying pan on the Boiling Plate.

PREPARING AHEAD Can be marinated up to a day ahead. Cook and serve immediately. Not suitable for freezing.

TIP Thread the prawns lengthways on to the skewers or cocktail sticks so they don't wobble about!

WONDERFUL SOUFFLÉ CROÛTONS

V

These are fantastic, so easy to make, and wonderful for nibbles to go with drinks. This batch makes about 100, so great to do for a large number of people. We were given this recipe by one of our Aga enthusiasts who is a caterer and has been to many of our Aga workshops. We thank her hugely.

75g (3 oz) full-fat cream cheese
150g (5 oz) butter
150g (5 oz) mature
    Cheddar, grated
2 large egg whites
salt and freshly ground
    black pepper
5 × 2.5cm (1 in) slices from
    a white tin loaf, 2–3 days
    old, crusts removed

Preheat the oven to 220°C/Fan 200°C/Gas 7. Line two or three baking sheets with non-stick baking paper or grease lightly.

STEP 1 Melt the cream cheese, butter and Cheddar in a pan over a low heat until completely melted (don't worry – the mixture looks very curdled at this stage). Whisk the egg whites until stiff, and carefully fold into the cheese mixture. Season lightly with salt and pepper.

STEP 2 Cut each slice of bread into four down, five across to give 20 × 2.5cm (1 in) cubes for each slice. Dip each cube into the soufflé mixture until completely coated and transfer to the prepared baking sheets.

STEP 3 Bake in the preheated oven for about 10 minutes until golden brown and puffed up. Turn over once and check after 6 minutes.

STEP 4 Serve at once.

AGA Slide the croûtons on the baking sheet directly on to the floor of the Roasting Oven and bake for 10–12 minutes, turning the croûtons over once, until golden brown and puffed up. Check after about 6 minutes as they can easily catch. Serve at once.

PREPARING AHEAD The croûtons freeze brilliantly. Freeze them raw at the end of step 2 on the baking sheet. When frozen, transfer to a polythene box and freeze for up to 1 month. Cook from frozen for about 5 minutes longer than the normal cooking time.

TIP When freezing the croûtons, write on the outside of the polythene bag or box how many it holds. This will help when defrosting to know how many they will serve.

HOISIN DUCK FILO BASKETS

These look stunning and taste delicious too.

1 duck breast, skinned
a little oil
salt and freshly ground
    black pepper
4 sheets of filo pastry, measuring
    38 × 26cm (15 × 10½ in)
25g (1 oz) butter, melted
about 8 tablespoons hoisin sauce
¼ small cucumber, seeds
    removed and finely diced
1 bunch of spring onions,
    finely chopped

Preheat the oven to 200°C/Fan 180°C/Gas 6 and grease two 12-hole mini muffin tins.

STEP 1 Heat a small frying pan until hot. Brush the duck breast with a little oil and season well. Brown in the pan until sealed and golden on both sides. Place on a baking sheet and roast in the preheated oven for 10 minutes. Leave to rest and then slice into tiny thin slices.

STEP 2 Meanwhile, brush two sheets of the filo pastry with melted butter and place one on top of the other. Slice 6 strips down and 4 strips across to make 24 squares (each square will have two layers of pastry). Place one square over another at an angle to make a star shape and then press this into the mini muffin tin (by now you should have four layers of pastry). Continue until all the squares have been used (this will make 12 tartlet cases). Repeat with the remaining sheets of filo.

STEP 3 Bake the cases in the oven for about 12 minutes until lightly golden brown and crisp. Leave to cool.

STEP 4 Put a little hoisin sauce in the base of each case, top with duck, cucumber and spring onions. Spoon a small blob of hoisin sauce on top.

STEP 5 Serve warm.

AGA Cook the duck and the pastry on the floor of the Roasting Oven for about 10 minutes.

PREPARING AHEAD Can be made up to 8 hours ahead and warmed to serve. The cooked filo cases freeze well in an airtight container.

TIP Hoisin sauce can be bought easily in supermarkets in the oriental section – it usually comes in a bottle or sachet.

MINI SAUSAGES WITH MANGO CHUTNEY AND SESAME

These are our favourite eats to do at any time of year. They are popular with all age groups, and if you want to be particularly clever, put wooden cocktail sticks in them, and stick them into a cottage loaf. You can reheat them and the loaf in the oven at the same time.

20 cocktail sausages
2 tablespoons mango chutney
25g (1 oz) sesame seeds

Preheat the oven to 200°C/Fan 180°C/Gas 6, or preheat the grill – whichever you prefer. Lightly grease a roasting tin or line the grill pan with foil.

STEP 1 Arrange the sausages in a roasting tin, in one layer.

STEP 2 Roast in the preheated oven for 20–30 minutes until golden brown and cooked through. Turn over halfway through.

STEP 3 Remove from the oven and tip into a bowl, making sure no excess fat from the pan is added. Stir in the mango chutney to coat the sausages.

STEP 4 Sprinkle over the sesame seeds, and serve the sausages warm with cocktail sticks.

AGA Slide the greased roasting tin on to the floor of the Roasting Oven and cook for about 15 minutes until golden brown and cooked through. Turn over halfway through.

PREPARING AHEAD These can be made up to a day ahead, reheated and sprinkled with sesame seeds to serve.

TIP Be sure to add the mango chutney while the sausages are hot so it sticks to them.

CHRISTMAS MULLED WINE

For an extra kick for a very special Christmas, add a glass
of sherry or brandy just before serving.

4 lemons
2 large oranges
2 bottles red wine
16 cloves
2 cinnamon sticks
about 150g (5 oz) caster sugar

STEP 1 Peel the zest very thinly from 3 lemons and 1 orange,
and squeeze the juice. Thinly slice the remaining orange
and lemon. Quarter the slices, put on a plate, cover and
reserve for garnish.

STEP 2 Pour the wine, 1.2 litres (2 pints) water, citrus
peel and juices into a large pan, and add the cloves and
cinnamon sticks. Bring to simmering point, cover and
keep at simmering for about an hour. Stir in sugar to taste.

STEP 3 Strain and serve hot with the reserved orange
and lemon slices floating on top.

AGA Bring to the boil on
the Boiling Plate, cover and
transfer to the Simmering
Oven for about an hour.

PREPARING AHEAD Can be
made, strained, cooled and kept
in covered containers in the fridge
for up to 3 days in advance. Add
the quartered lemon and orange
slices just before serving.

TIP Use a ladle to serve the wine
– this makes it a lot quicker!

FIRST COURSES

CHAPTER TWO

The first course is the introduction to the meal, so it must look good and taste good, and you have to remember that your guests will probably be hungry! Cold first courses are useful for the cook because they can be prepared in advance (kept in the fridge, clingfilmed), but at this time of year, when the weather is cold, something hot might be much more appropriate. However, many hot first courses can have been prepared in advance, too, only needing a quick heat through on the hob or in the oven or Aga. Soups, for instance, can have been made and frozen a month or so in advance. All you need to do is defrost overnight, then heat. And there are many other hot ideas here which won't take too long to put together: try the Haddock and Spinach Pots, the Stilton and Leek Tarts, or the Roasted Beetroot and Goat's Cheese Bruschetta.

Some of the first courses here might seem a little complicated, but, as the preparation is divided up into separate stages, it won't be too much of a chore. 'Smart' recipes such as the Salmon and Dill Terrines and the Prawn and Avocado Tians take time to make, but I can assure you they are worth it in terms of look and taste. But if you are really strapped for time, you could opt for assembly jobs: I'm thinking of recipes such as the Asparagus and Quail's Egg Salad, or the Antipasti of Smoked Fish and Prawns. There's something for everyone here!

Always serve hot rolls or bread and butter with first courses. Garlic or herb bread could have been frozen, ready just to heat through in the oven at the last minute.

STILTON AND LEEK TARTS

V

Make these in two Yorkshire pudding tins, each of which will make four individual tarts. It is essential to roll the pastry thinly, then line the tins with the circles of pastry to come just above the rims. Instead of making your own cheese pastry, use a 500g (18 oz) pack of bought shortcrust pastry if time is short. Serve with a salad if liked.

CHEESE PASTRY
175g (6 oz) plain flour
¼ teaspoon salt
1 teaspoon English
mustard powder
75g (3 oz) butter, cut
into small pieces
50g (2 oz) Parmesan,
freshly grated
1 egg, beaten

FILLING
a good knob of butter
1 large leek, weighing about
350g (12 oz), trimmed,
washed and finely sliced
100g (4 oz) Stilton cheese,
coarsely grated
a large handful of fresh
parsley, coarsely chopped
2 eggs
300ml (½ pint) single cream
a little freshly grated nutmeg
salt and freshly ground
black pepper
12 black olives, stoned
and halved (optional)

STEP 1 First make the pastry. Measure the flour, salt, mustard and butter into the processor or a bowl, and process or rub in until the mixture resembles fine breadcrumbs. Add the Parmesan and beaten egg and mix again as long as it takes for the ingredients to come together. Chill for 30 minutes wrapped in clingfilm.

STEP 2 For the filling, heat the butter in a large non-stick pan and add the sliced leek. Cover and cook over a low heat for about 15 minutes to soften. Return to a high heat to drive off any excess liquid.

Preheat the oven to 200°C/Fan 180°C/Gas 6.

STEP 3 Roll the pastry out thinly on a lightly floured work surface and, using an 11cm (4½ in) cutter, cut into eight discs. Use these to line two Yorkshire pudding trays. Chill if time allows.

STEP 4 Bake the pastry blind in the preheated oven for 15 minutes, removing the paper and beans for the last 5 minutes. Reduce the temperature to 180°C/Fan 160°C/Gas 4.

Recipe continued overleaf

Recipe continued

STEP 5 Divide the cooled leek between the pastry-lined Yorkshire pudding tins, and top with grated cheese and chopped parsley. Beat the eggs and add the cream, nutmeg and some seasoning. Carefully pour the egg and cream mixture into the tartlets and top each one with a few halved olives if liked.

STEP 6 Bake in the reduced-temperature oven for 15–20 minutes until the filling is set and beginning to colour.

AGA For the filling, heat the butter on the Boiling Plate, and cook the sliced leek for a few minutes. Cover, transfer to the floor of the Simmering Oven and leave for 15–20 minutes until soft. Return to the Boiling Plate to drive off any excess liquid. You don't need to blind-bake the pastry in the Aga: simply fill the raw pastry cases and bake on the grid shelf on the floor of the Roasting Oven for 15–20 minutes. If the pastry needs a little more browning underneath, remove the grid shelf and put the tins directly on the floor for a few minutes.

PREPARING AHEAD Line the Yorkshire pudding tins with pastry ahead of time. Cover and keep in the fridge. Prepare and chop the filling ingredients. Or you could freeze the freshly baked tarts, once cold, for up to 2 months. To reheat, thaw and bake in a moderate oven for about 10–15 minutes or until hot.

TIP Substitute 1 large white onion, finely sliced, for the leek if liked. Use it in exactly the same way as in the main recipe.

BUTTERNUT SQUASH SOUP

V

Unlike pumpkins, butternut squashes are available all year. Roasting them first in the oven means that you don't have to tackle removing the tough skin, and it fills the kitchen with a delicious aroma! The soup freezes well too.

3 small butternut squashes,
    about 1.6kg (3½ lb) total weight
about 2 tablespoons olive oil
salt and freshly ground
    black pepper
freshly grated nutmeg
25g (1 oz) butter
1 large onion, roughly chopped
2 large carrots, roughly chopped
2 large celery sticks, sliced
2.5cm (1 in) piece fresh root
    ginger, grated
1.2–1.3 litres (2–2¼ pints)
    vegetable stock
leaves from 1 small sprig
    of fresh rosemary, chopped

Preheat the oven to 200°C/Fan 180°C/Gas 6.

STEP 1 Cut the butternut squashes in half lengthways, scoop out the seeds with a metal spoon and discard. Arrange the squash halves cut-side up in a roasting tin just big enough to hold them in a single layer, and drizzle over the olive oil. Season each squash half with salt, pepper and freshly grated nutmeg. Pour 150ml (¼ pint) water around the squash. Roast in the preheated oven for about an hour or until tender. Allow to cool.

STEP 2 Melt the butter in a large pan and add the onion, carrot, celery and grated ginger. Cook over a high heat for a few minutes, stirring continuously. Add the stock, rosemary and seasoning, and bring to the boil for a few minutes. Cover and continue to cook over simmering heat for about 20 minutes until the vegetables are tender.

STEP 3 When cool enough to handle, scoop the flesh from the squash skins and add to the pan. Blend the vegetables in a liquidiser or food processor until smooth. (If you use a food processor, it is easier to process the vegetables with a little of the liquid, adding the remaining liquid to the processed vegetables to make the soup.)

STEP 4 Taste for seasoning and serve hot with crusty bread.

AGA Slide the squash halves in a roasting tin on to the second set of runners of the Roasting Oven for about an hour, basting occasionally, until very tender. To cook the vegetables, bring to the boil on the Boiling Plate, then cover and transfer to the Simmering Oven for about 20 minutes.

PREPARING AHEAD Make a lot of this in advance – especially if you have squashes growing in the garden – and freeze in suitable quantities.

TIP This recipe can also be made with pumpkin. Just cut into large chunks and roast in the preheated oven as above.

ROASTED VEG WITH GOAT'S CHEESE

V

This starter looks stunning, and all the preparation can be done the day before. I like the peppers peeled but it is not essential. If you don't like goat's cheese, the vegetables are delicious topped with Parma ham and shavings of Parmesan.

1 aubergine, halved lengthways
2 small courgettes
2 red peppers, halved
 and deseeded
olive oil
1 tablespoon balsamic vinegar
a pinch of fresh thyme
 leaves, chopped
1 fat garlic clove, cut in half
salt and freshly ground
 black pepper
2 × 100g (4 oz) Capricorn
 goat's cheeses (a roll
 shape, with skin on)
4 tablespoons fresh
 white breadcrumbs
paprika

STEP 1 Slice the aubergine and courgettes on the diagonal, about 0.5 cm (¼ in) thick.

STEP 2 Put the peppers skin-side up under a hot grill, about 10cm (4 in) away from the heat, and grill until the skins scorch and blacken. Put the hot peppers in a plastic bag, seal the top and allow to sweat. When the peppers are cool enough to handle, peel the skin off and slice the flesh neatly.

STEP 3 Mix the aubergine, courgette and 1 tablespoon oil together in a large plastic bag or bowl. Heat a ridged grill pan or frying pan. When the pan is very hot, char-grill the aubergine and courgettes in batches until tender (turn only once). Transfer to a bowl, add the sliced red pepper, 2 tablespoons of oil, the vinegar, thyme and garlic. Season well.

STEP 4 Remove the ends from the cheeses, leaving the skin around the sides, and cut each cheese into three even discs. Brush the cheese with a little olive oil and roll the cheese in seasoned breadcrumbs, to give a fine coating. Place on a piece of non-stick paper on a baking sheet.

Preheat the oven to 200°C/Fan 180°C/Gas 6.

STEP 5 About 15 minutes before serving, put the vegetables in a serving dish, cover tightly with foil and put into the preheated oven to warm through.

Recipe continued overleaf

Recipe continued

STEP 6 About 5 minutes prior to assembling, increase the oven temperature to 220°C/Fan 200°C/Gas 7. Sprinkle the cheese with paprika and slide on to the top shelf of the oven for about 5 minutes until just beginning to melt around the edges but still firm in the middle (these do melt quite a lot – this is part of the charm!).

STEP 7 Remove the garlic from the vegetables and spoon the hot vegetables on to six individual plates. With a fish slice, lift a slice of warmed goat's cheese on to each pile of vegetables. Drizzle the dressing from the vegetables around the plate. Serve with warm ciabatta bread.

AGA Scorch the red peppers on non-stick paper on a baking tray at the very top of the Roasting Oven for about 20 minutes, or until black, then follow the rest of step 2. To finish and assemble, reheat the vegetables in the Simmering Oven, 15 minutes before serving. Heat the cheese on the second set of runners in the Roasting Oven for 3–5 minutes, until just beginning to melt.

PREPARING AHEAD Prepare the char-grilled vegetables, continuing to the end of step 3, and marinate overnight in the fridge. The coated cheese may also be left on non-stick paper or foil in the fridge overnight, covered in clingfilm.

TIP To get attractive ridges on meat, fish, vegetables, etc. when char-grilling, you need a ridged grill pan (most of them are non-stick). First butter or oil the food being roasted and season with salt and pepper. Heat the pan until very hot, then add the food to the pan until cooked.

LEEK AND STILTON SOUP

V

This is a winter soup essentially, but perfect for using up the Stilton that is always left over at Christmas. You will see that I suggest coarsely grating the Stilton. I find crumbling unsatisfactory, as it is sticky and gets under the nails! It is worth infusing the milk, if you have time, with the bay leaves and nutmeg.

350g (12 oz) leeks
600ml (1 pint) milk
2 bay leaves
a little freshly grated nutmeg
75g (3 oz) butter
75g (3 oz) plain flour
1.2 litres (2 pints) stock
salt and freshly ground
    black pepper
150g (5 oz) Stilton cheese,
    crumbled
a little single cream
fresh chopped parsley
    or chives

STEP 1 Cut the leeks into four lengthways and shred finely on the diagonal. Wash and drain thoroughly.

STEP 2 Measure the milk into a small saucepan, heat until hand hot over a low heat, then add the bay leaves and a grating of nutmeg. Cover the pan and simmer very gently to infuse the flavours for about 10 minutes.

STEP 3 Melt the butter in a pan, add the flour and cook for a few moments. Add the strained hot milk, stirring well, then add the stock. Stir in the leeks, season (using very little salt because of the salty cheese) and bring to the boil. Simmer for a few minutes, then add the cheese and stir well. Cover and simmer over a low heat for 15 minutes until the leeks are tender.

STEP 4 Check the seasoning. If the soup is a little too thick, thin down with milk or stock. Served with a little added single cream, and garnish with freshly chopped parsley or chives.

AGA At step 3, cover, bring to the boil and transfer to the Simmering Oven for about 15 minutes or until the leeks are tender.

PREPARING AHEAD The soup can be made, quickly cooled and stored in the fridge for up to 2 days. You could also cool, pack and freeze the soup at the end of step 3 for up to 1 month.

TIP It is really worthwhile infusing the milk, if you have time, with the bay leaves and nutmeg, as it gives a lovely flavour to the milk.

ROASTED BEETROOT AND GOAT'S CHEESE BRUSCHETTA

V

A delicious starter, one which can be made ahead and popped in the oven to serve. Balsamic glaze can be bought from most delis and supermarkets.

2 medium beetroot, raw
olive oil
salt and freshly ground
    black pepper
2 x 100g (4 oz) Capricorn
    goat's cheese (a roll shape)
½ x part-baked ciabatta loaf
1 x 85g (3 oz) packet rocket,
    lamb's lettuce or watercress
salad dressing, to serve

RED ONION MARMALADE
2 tablespoons olive oil
3 large red onions, thinly sliced
1 tablespoon brown sugar
1 tablespoon fresh thyme
    leaves, chopped
1 tablespoon balsamic glaze

Preheat the oven to 200 ºC/Fan 180º/Gas 6. Line a baking sheet with non-stick paper.

STEP 1 To make the red onion marmalade measure the oil into a frying pan, add the red onions and stir over a high heat for 3–4 minutes. Cover with a lid, lower the heat and simmer for 15 minutes or until completely soft. Remove the lid and increase the heat. Add the sugar and thyme and fry until the onions have caramelised and there is no liquid in the pan. Finally stir in the balsamic glaze and set aside.

STEP 2 Meanwhile, peel the raw beetroot (using gloves) and cut into 1cm (½ in) dice. Toss the cubes in 2 tablespoons of oil and season. Scatter over the prepared baking sheet and roast in the oven for 25 minutes until lightly golden.

STEP 3 Slice each roll of goat's cheese into three even discs and cut the ciabatta into six 2cm (¾ in) slices. Brush the bread with a little olive oil on one side and arrange oiled-side down along one side of a separate baking sheet.

STEP 4 Bake the ciabatta in the oven for 5 minutes. Remove from the oven and add the goat's cheese slices to the empty side of the baking sheet. Put back into the oven for 10 minutes or until the bread is lightly golden and the cheese is just melting.

STEP 5 Arrange the bruschetta on a large plate and spoon some onion marmalade on top of each slice. Sit the warm goat's cheese on top of this and then prepare the salad leaves. Toss them in a little dressing and then place a handful on top of the cheese.

STEP 6 Arrange the roasted beetroot around the bruschetta and drizzle some olive oil and balsamic glaze around the edge of the plate. Serve immediately.

AGA Make the onion marmalade in the Simmering Oven. Roast the beetroot on the floor of the Roasting Oven for 25 minutes. Toast the bruschetta on the floor of the Roasting Oven for 5 minutes. Add the goat's cheese and slide to the top of the Roasting Oven for 7 minutes or until golden and the cheese is starting to melt.

PREPARING AHEAD The onion marmalade can be made up to 3 days ahead and reheated to serve. The beetroot can be roasted ahead and reheated to serve. Have the ciabatta arranged on the baking sheet and cook to serve. Not suitable for freezing.

TIP If you put the goat's cheese into the freezer for 30 minutes it makes it much easier to slice.

FRESH SALMON AND DILL TERRINES

These terrines are impressive and very easy to make – no gelatine!
Don't expect them to set firm; it is a soft and light consistency.
They can be made a day ahead in small round or oval ramekins.
Serve with brown bread and butter.

350g (12 oz) fresh salmon
fillet (boned weight)
salt and freshly ground
black pepper
6 small sprigs of fresh dill
plus 2 extra tablespoons
chopped fresh dill
3 slices smoked salmon
6 tablespoons 'light'
low-calorie mayonnaise
6 tablespoons full-fat
crème fraîche
juice of ½ lemon

TO SERVE
a few salad leaves, dressed
6 lemon wedges

Preheat the oven to 160ºC/Fan 140ºC/Gas 3.

STEP 1 Season the fresh salmon with salt and pepper
and wrap in a layer of buttered foil. Slide on to a baking
sheet and bake in the preheated oven until just opaque,
15–20 minutes. Remove any skin (but keep any juice).
Allow to cool to lukewarm.

STEP 2 Wet the inside of six small ramekins and line with
clingfilm. Place a sprig of dill in the base of each and cut
six discs of smoked salmon to fit neatly into the base on
top of the dill. (If there is not enough smoked salmon to
make six complete discs, use the odd pieces to form circles.)
Use the base of the ramekin on top of the slice of smoked
salmon to judge the size of a circle.

STEP 3 Flake the remaining cold salmon fillet, removing
any bones. Mix the salmon and any cooking juices with the
mayonnaise and crème fraîche in a bowl, and season with
the extra dill, lemon juice, salt and pepper. Taste and add
more seasoning if necessary. Divide evenly between the
ramekins and cover with any overhanging clingfilm. Allow
to set in the fridge for about 12 hours, preferably overnight.

STEP 4 The next day turn out on to a few dressed salad
leaves, and garnish with the lemon wedges.

AGA Cook the salmon for about
8 minutes in the Roasting Oven
on the lowest set of runners.

PREPARING AHEAD Completely
make up to 2 days ahead, and
keep in the fridge. Turn out up
to 2 hours ahead and keep in the
fridge until just before serving.

TIP If you only have full-fat
mayonnaise in the fridge,
this works well too.

ASPARAGUS AND QUAIL'S EGG SALAD

This attractive plate of salad is light and tempting. You could swap some of the ingredients: salmon for prawns, and perhaps add some dressed artichoke hearts.

12 quail's eggs
18 short asparagus spears or, if large, 9 cut in half lengthways (cut off the very woody ends)
2 tablespoons 'light' low-calorie mayonnaise
2 tablespoons half-fat crème fraîche
1 heaped teaspoon finely chopped fresh chives
1 heaped teaspoon finely chopped fresh parsley
salt and freshly ground black pepper
6 slices smoked salmon
1 lemon, cut into 6 wedges

STEP 1 Bring the quail's eggs to the boil in cold water and boil for a further 3 minutes. Drain, run under cold water and peel.

STEP 2 Cook the asparagus in boiling water for 4–5 minutes until just tender. Drain and refresh thoroughly in very cold water.

STEP 3 Measure the mayonnaise, crème fraîche and herbs into a bowl. Season well with salt and pepper.

STEP 4 Arrange a slice of smoked salmon around the edge of each starter plate, spoon the mayonnaise mixture next to the smoked salmon, and top with 4 quail's egg halves and 3 asparagus tips. Serve with a lemon wedge and brown bread.

PREPARING AHEAD If you have room in your fridge, assemble completely on individual plates, cover tightly and keep in the fridge for up to 12 hours. Or complete steps 1–3, cover and keep in the fridge for up to 6 hours.

TIP See page 62 for some tips on how to make peeling quail's eggs easier. Keep fresh herbs in the fridge, so useful to have to hand for garnishing, or to chop into pasta or salad at the last minute. Put in a jug with a little water, with a plastic bag over the top to keep fresh. Basil, a herb that is accustomed to a warm climate, is best kept *out* of the fridge.

GRAVADLAX

Gravadlax is a classic Scandinavian recipe for pickled fresh salmon. It is not difficult to prepare and is a really special first course. Ask your fishmonger to bone a whole salmon for you, leaving you with two large fillets with the skin on.

1 × 1.8kg (4 lb) whole fresh
    salmon, filleted to give
    you 2 sides
fresh sprigs of dill, lemon
    wedges and rye bread to serve

PICKLING INGREDIENTS
4 tablespoons dried dill
masses of freshly ground
    black pepper
4 tablespoons caster sugar
2 tablespoons coarse sea salt

MUSTARD DILL SAUCE
3 tablespoons Dijon mustard
2 tablespoons caster sugar
1 tablespoon white wine vinegar
1 egg yolk
150ml (¼ pint) sunflower oil
salt and freshly ground
    black pepper
2 tablespoons chopped fresh
    dill or 1 tablespoon dried

STEP 1 Lay the salmon fillets alongside each other, skin-side down, on a board. Sprinkle each fillet evenly with the dried dill, then masses of freshly ground black pepper, then the sugar and salt, pressing each ingredient in well, using the palm of your hand.

STEP 2 Sandwich the fillets together, skin-side out, to re-form the fish, and wrap in a double layer of foil. Put this into a large polythene bag and seal. Check that the salmon fillets are still on top of one another, then lay in a large dish, put another large dish on top and stack kitchen weights, or heavy cans, on top of that. Keep the dish in the fridge for 24 hours to allow the salmon to marinate, turning it after 12 hours. (I usually start to marinate the salmon in the evening and then it is ready to be turned in the morning.)

STEP 3 To make the sauce, whisk together the mustard, sugar, vinegar and egg yolk, then gradually whisk in the oil. The sauce should have the consistency of mayonnaise. Add salt and pepper to taste and stir in the dill.

STEP 4 After 24 hours unwrap the gravadlax. A lot of salty, sticky liquid will have leaked out – this is quite normal. Remove the fish from the pickling liquid, which can now be discarded. Separate the fillets.

STEP 5 To serve, slice each fillet at an angle of about 45 degrees, cutting the flesh away from the skin. The slices should be slightly thicker than for smoked salmon, and each slice should be edged with dill.

PREPARING AHEAD Before slicing, the gravadlax will keep in the fridge, wrapped in clingfilm, for up to a week. After slicing, the slices of gravadlax will sit happily arranged on serving plates for up to about 6 hours, as long as they are covered with clingfilm and kept chilled. The mustard dill sauce can also be made about 6 hours ahead and kept tightly covered in a bowl or sealed jar in the fridge. Gravadlax freezes extremely well. Wrap the separate halves of the marinated gravadlax tightly in clingfilm, seal and label, and freeze for up to 2 months. Part-thaw the salmon for about 1 hour before slicing. It is best not to freeze the mustard dill sauce as it tends to curdle when thawed.

PRAWN AND AVOCADO TIANS

A very impressive first course. These are made in metal rings bought from Lakeland Limited or good cook shops (you need six rings of 7cm/2¾ in diameter). You could also use ramekin dishes lined with clingfilm.

4 medium tomatoes
3 small avocados, firm
    but just ripe
juice of about ½ lemon
1 tablespoon salad dressing
salt and freshly ground
    black pepper
2 spring onions, very finely sliced
175g (6 oz) cooked tiger
    prawns, shelled
2 generous tablespoons 'light'
    low-calorie mayonnaise
2 good teaspoons creamed
    horseradish

TO SERVE
lightly dressed green salad
    leaves, including rocket
    or lamb's lettuce
chopped fresh parsley

STEP 1 First, dip the tomatoes in boiling water for 10 seconds. Plunge into cold water and remove skins. Quarter each tomato, remove the seeds and slice the flesh into thin strips.

STEP 2 Cut the avocados in half, remove the stones and peel. Cut each half into small chunks and tip half into a bowl. Mash together with the lemon juice. Stir in the rest of the chunks.

STEP 3 Place a piece of clingfilm on a flat tray and stand your rings on top. Divide the avocado chunks between the rings. Press down firmly using a small ramekin that fits inside the ring. Add the tomato and salad dressing to the empty bowl, season with salt and pepper and add the spring onions. Spoon on top of the avocado. Press down again.

STEP 4 In the same now empty bowl, mix the prawns, mayonnaise, horseradish and some salt and pepper. Spoon the prawns on top of the tomato (they will come slightly over the top of the ring). Cover the tray and rings with clingfilm, and chill for at least 4 hours.

STEP 5 Arrange some dressed green salad leaves on six plates. Lift a ring into the centre of each plate using a palette knife or fish slice. Carefully remove the ring. Sprinkle the prawns with parsley. Serve with warm rolls.

PREPARING AHEAD The tians can be made the day before, kept in the fridge and turned out on the day, a couple of hours in advance of serving. Keep in the fridge, though.

TIP Instead of prawns, use the same weight of flaked cooked salmon or crab. Make sure you use creamed horseradish for this recipe and not a hot horseradish sauce, or the flavour will overpower the prawns. It is wise to taste the horseradish cream and cut down the amount if necessary.

ANTIPASTI OF SMOKED FISH AND PRAWNS

This is a great idea for when time is short and you want a smart but simple lunch. Serve with good warm bread or rolls and butter.

12 quail's eggs
1 × 275g (10 oz) jar herrings in dill marinade, drained
1 × 200g (7 oz) packet smoked mackerel fillets
6 smoked salmon slices
6 cooked Madagascan prawns, shell on
1 × 50g bag mixed salad leaves or pea shoots
1 lemon, cut into 6 wedges

HORSERADISH AND DILL SAUCE
6 tablespoons half-fat crème fraîche
2 tablespoons creamed horseradish
2 tablespoons snipped fresh dill
salt and freshly ground black pepper

STEP 1 Put the quail's eggs in a saucepan. Cover with cold water, bring up to the boil then simmer for 3 minutes. Drain, refresh in cold water and peel.

STEP 2 For the sauce, mix the crème fraîche, horseradish and dill together in a small bowl, and season well.

STEP 3 Put the quail's eggs, sauce and herrings into three separate small bowls, scallop shells or ramekins, and arrange in a triangle shape near the centre of a large round plate.

STEP 4 Skin the mackerel, then flake into large pieces and arrange next to the sauce.

STEP 5 Arrange the smoked salmon and prawns in the remaining gaps.

STEP 6 Place the mixed salad in a pile in the middle of the plate. Garnish with the lemon wedges.

PREPARING AHEAD The sauce can be made up to 2 days ahead and kept, covered, in the fridge. The antipasti platter can be prepared 4 hours ahead if kept covered and chilled.

TIP Quail's eggs are difficult to peel if very fresh, so buy them a week ahead and keep them in the fridge. They're sometimes difficult to peel once boiled, too, like fresh hen eggs, as the white part of the egg clings to the shell. It helps if you peel them straightaway once they are cool enough to handle, so plunge into cold water after the 3 minutes' boiling and get peeling!

SMOKED HADDOCK BOUILLABAISSE

A good substantial soup, a meal in itself served with lots of crusty bread and a salad to follow. I have used full-fat milk to give a good creamy flavour. Add a little cream before serving if you use a low-fat milk.

50g (2 oz) butter
4–6 spring onions, thinly sliced
6 celery sticks, sliced
2 medium carrots, chopped into 1cm (½ in) dice
450g (1 lb) old potatoes, peeled and cut into 2cm (¾ in) chunks
40g (1½ oz) plain flour
600ml (1 pint) fish or vegetable stock
600ml (1 pint) full-fat milk
salt and freshly ground black pepper
700g (1½ lb) undyed smoked haddock, skinned and chopped into bite-sized pieces
chopped fresh dill to garnish

STEP 1 Heat the butter in a large pan. Add the prepared spring onions, celery and carrot, stir to coat the vegetables in the butter, then cover and cook gently for about 3 minutes until beginning to soften. Add the potato and cook for a further 1–2 minutes.

STEP 2 Add the flour to the vegetables, stir, then add the stock and milk. Add black pepper to taste, but no salt at this stage as the fish is very salty. Bring to the boil, cover and simmer until the vegetables are tender, 10–15 minutes.

STEP 3 Add the haddock to the vegetable mixture in the pan and simmer gently for a couple of minutes until the fish is cooked.

STEP 4 Adjust the seasoning and garnish with dill.

AGA Start on the Boiling Plate. When the vegetables and liquid are added, cover and bring to the boil. Transfer to the Simmering Oven and cook for about 15 minutes until the vegetables are tender. Add the haddock and simmer on the Simmering Plate for a few minutes. Continue with the recipe.

PREPARING AHEAD Complete the soup but don't add the garnish yet. Cool, pour into a suitable container and keep in the fridge for 24 hours.

TIP Be careful not to boil the bouillabaisse after adding the fish – just simmer gently, otherwise the fish will break up.

HADDOCK AND SPINACH POTS

An uncomplicated yet impressive first course of individual ramekins with fresh spinach, smoked haddock and some creamy, cheesy sauce. Serve them with really fresh rolls or bread.

300g (10 oz) fresh
   spinach, washed
salt and freshly ground
   black pepper
freshly grated nutmeg
butter to grease
300g (10 oz) undyed smoked
   haddock, skinned
150ml (¼ pint) double cream
1 teaspoon grain mustard
45g (1½ oz) mature
   Cheddar, grated
paprika

Preheat the oven to 220ºC/Fan 200ºC/Gas 7.

STEP 1 Wilt the spinach in a large saucepan without water, stirring frequently until it has all collapsed. Tip into a colander and squeeze out as much liquid as possible. Dry off with kitchen paper until very dry.

STEP 2 Roughly chop the spinach and season with pepper and grated nutmeg. Divide between the bases of six buttered ramekins. Arrange the ramekins on a baking tray.

STEP 3 Cut the smoked haddock into small chunks and arrange on top of the spinach.

STEP 4 Mix the cream and mustard together and season with pepper and a little salt. Spoon over the fish and sprinkle with grated cheese.

STEP 5 Dust with paprika and bake in the preheated oven for 12–15 minutes until bubbling and golden brown.

AGA To bake the ramekins, slide the baking sheet with the pots on to the top set of runners in the Roasting Oven for 12–15 minutes.

PREPARING AHEAD
Bring everything together up to 12 hours ahead, and cook to serve.

TIP There's no need to use baby spinach; use ordinary spinach or Swiss chard, and remove the stalks.

CARLTON PÂTÉ

Chicken livers are very reasonable to buy. This smooth, tasty pâté makes a good first course, especially if serving fish as a main. Any left over may be used as a sandwich filling.

225g (8 oz) fresh chicken livers
225g (8 oz) butter, softened
1 small onion, finely chopped
350g (12 oz) button
   mushrooms, sliced
50g (2 oz) fresh breadcrumbs
lots of freshly grated nutmeg
175g (6 oz) full-fat cream cheese
2 teaspoons lemon juice
1 scant tablespoon soy sauce
1 tablespoon chopped
   fresh parsley
salt and freshly ground
   black pepper

STEP 1 Trim the chicken livers, removing any membrane. Melt 75g (3 oz) of the butter in a large non-stick frying pan over a high heat and sauté the chicken livers until lightly cooked but still pink in the middle. Lift out of the pan and set aside. Add the onion to the pan, stir, then simmer over a low heat for about 15 minutes until soft.

STEP 2 Add the mushrooms to the onion and fry briskly over high heat for a few minutes. Stir in the breadcrumbs and allow to cool.

STEP 3 Purée the mushroom mixture with the chicken livers in the processor. Add the remaining butter, the nutmeg, cream cheese, lemon juice, soy sauce and parsley, and purée again until evenly blended. Season well, and taste.

STEP 4 Turn into a pâté dish or small terrine and chill in the fridge before serving with toasted French bread.

AGA Fry the livers in a pan on the Boiling Plate, remove and set aside. Fry the onion for a couple of minutes on the Boiling Plate, cover, then transfer to the Simmering Oven for about 15 minutes or until the onion is soft. Add the mushrooms and fry on the Boiling Plate, then continue as above.

PREPARING AHEAD This pâté will keep, covered in the fridge, for up to 3 days. It will also freeze. Cover and freeze for up to 3 months.

TIP Be sure to use full-fat cream cheese in this recipe – half-fat will make the pâté too soft.

CHRISTMAS TURKEY SOUP

Perfect soup for using the carcass of the turkey and any turkey meat left over from Christmas Day.

25g (1 oz) butter
2 leeks, thinly sliced
1 large carrot, peeled
    and thinly sliced
1 medium parsnip, peeled
    and thinly sliced
25g (1 oz) plain flour
1.2 litres (2 pints) hot homemade
    turkey stock (see page 108)
salt and freshly ground
    black pepper
75g (3 oz) cooked turkey,
    sliced into small pieces

STEP 1 Melt the butter in a large saucepan. Add the leeks, carrot and parsnip and stir over a gentle heat for 3–4 minutes until the vegetables are starting to soften.

STEP 2 Sprinkle in the flour and coat the vegetables. Pour in the hot stock, stirring until thickened slightly.

STEP 3 Cover with a lid and bring up to the boil. Season with salt and pepper, lower the heat and simmer for about 20 minutes until all of the vegetables are tender.

STEP 4 Stir in the cooked turkey, check seasoning and serve.

AGA Bring to the boil on the Boiling Plate, cover and transfer to the Simmering Oven for 20 minutes or until the vegetables are tender.

PREPARING AHEAD If using freshly made stock, this can be made up to a day ahead and reheated. Freezes well.

TIP This soup should be made within a couple of days of roasting the turkey so the meat is still fresh.

FISH AND VEGETARIAN

CHAPTER THREE

Fish is often forgotten at Christmas time, primarily because it has to be bought and cooked when fresh. This is why there are fewer recipes in this chapter than there are elsewhere. However, fish is so good to eat, and so good for us, that I have included some old favourites, including My Family Fish Pie. This is the ultimate comfort food and would, I think, be perfect for a Christmas Eve supper.

When planning to cook fish at Christmas, order it well in advance from your fishmonger or supermarket, collect and cook it at the last minute. The recipes in this chapter are on the lighter side and they are a welcome change from the traditional Christmas roasts and casseroles.

And don't forget about the smoked and preserved fish you can buy: smoked salmon and trout can be served in some fashion as canapés or starters, and you could try my gravadlax recipe in the previous chapter, a perfect first course or a light supper after a heavy lunch.

I've also given you a couple of recipes for any vegetarian guests you might be entertaining over Christmas. Often people who don't eat meat have to rely on an omelette, or a plate of the vegetables that you are serving with the meat, which can be a bit boring. I think it's nice to cook them something a little more special – particularly the Aubergine Five-nut Roast on page 93 – and the recipes here are so delicious that we often treat ourselves to them at lunchtime, and don't miss the meat at all.

MY FAMILY FISH PIE

A good fish pie is perfect for the family on Christmas Eve, and is an ideal dish to prepare ahead. You could add celeriac or parsnip to the potato and cook in the same way – your family either love or hate parsnips and celeriac but it does make an interesting addition to the normal plain mashed potato.

75g (3 oz) butter, plus extra
   for greasing
1 large onion, roughly chopped
50g (2 oz) plain flour
600ml (1 pint) milk
salt and freshly ground
   black pepper
2 tablespoons lemon juice
350g (12 oz) fresh haddock,
   cut into 1cm/½ in pieces
350g (12 oz) smoked undyed
   haddock, cut into 1cm/
   ½ in pieces
4 hard-boiled free-range
   eggs, roughly chopped

TOPPING
900g (2 lb) potatoes, peeled
   and cut into even-sized pieces
about 8 tablespoons hot milk
about 50g (2 oz) butter

Preheat the oven to 200°C/Fan 180°C/Gas 6 and grease a shallow 2.5 litre (4½ pint) ovenproof dish, approximately 30 × 23cm (12 × 9 in), using a little extra butter.

STEP 1 Melt the butter in a pan on a high heat and fry the onion for a few minutes. Lower the heat, cover and leave to soften for 15 minutes.

STEP 2 Remove the lid and increase the heat to remove any moisture. Sprinkle in the flour and then add the milk gradually, stirring well and allowing the sauce to thicken until all the milk has been added.

STEP 3 Season with salt and freshly ground black pepper, add the lemon juice and raw fish and cook for a couple of minutes, stirring continuously until the fish has just cooked. Stir in the smoked haddock. Pour the mixture into the buttered dish and leave to cool. Top with the hard-boiled eggs.

STEP 4 For the topping, boil the potatoes in a pan of salted water until tender. Drain, tip the potatoes back into the pan, add milk and butter and mash until lump-free. Use a ricer to get a smooth mash, if you have one. Add salt and freshly ground black pepper to taste. Pipe the mash in diagonal swirls over the fish in the dish or spread over carefully and score with a fork.

STEP 5 Bake in the preheated oven for about 30 minutes, or until the potato is crisp and golden brown.

AGA Cook the sauce on the Simmering Plate, then bake the pie in the Roasting Oven on the third set of runners for 30–35 minutes until the potato topping is golden and the pie piping hot.

PREPARING AHEAD The pie can be prepared ahead to the end of step 5. Cover with clingfilm and keep in the fridge for up to 24 hours before cooking as directed. It is best not to freeze the fish pie as hard-boiled eggs and mashed potato do not freeze particularly well.

TIP Other white fish can be substituted for the haddock, such as hake or cod (make sure it has been caught sustainably). Anchovy sauce adds a depth of flavour to the pie, and is usually available in the special ingredients section of good supermarkets.

BAKED SALMON WITH PARMESAN CRUST

This recipe in one of my all-time favourites, and is a perfect fish recipe to prepare ahead. It allows the sauce to become really cold and firm before oven baking. If it is a very special occasion – perhaps Christmas Eve – and you like a lot of sauce, double up on the amount. See the Tip for a less rich sauce alternative.

6 ×150g (5 oz) centre-cut
    salmon fillets, skinned
salt and freshly ground
    black pepper
butter
paprika
chopped fresh parsley

SAUCE
75ml (2½ fl oz) white wine
175g (6 oz) chestnut
    mushrooms, sliced
300ml (½ pint) double cream

TOPPING
25g (1 oz) fresh white
    breadcrumbs
25g (1 oz) Parmesan,
    coarsely grated
2 tablespoons chopped
    fresh parsley
grated rind of ½ lemon
paprika

Preheat the oven to 220ºC/Fan 200ºC/Gas 7.

STEP 1 Season both sides of the salmon fillets and place on a buttered baking sheet or roasting tin.

STEP 2 Measure the wine and mushrooms into a pan, and boil over high heat for 1 minute. Lift out the mushrooms with a slotted spoon, and reduce the wine to about 2 tablespoons. Add the cream, bring to the boil and reduce to a sauce consistency. Season. Return the mushrooms to the sauce and leave to cool completely.

STEP 3 Mix the topping ingredients together in a bowl.

STEP 4 Spoon a little of the cold mushroom mixture on each salmon fillet, but do not spread to the edge. Sprinkle the breadcrumb topping over the mushroom mixture and dust with paprika. Save the rest of the sauce, to reheat and serve separately.

STEP 5 Bake in the preheated oven for about 15 minutes. When the salmon is done, it will have changed from translucent to an opaque pink. Sprinkle with more chopped parsley, and serve immediately, with the reheated sauce.

AGA Bake on the grid shelf on the floor of the Roasting Oven for 10–15 minutes.

PREPARING AHEAD Complete steps 1—4, cover with clingfilm and keep in the fridge for up to 24 hours.

TIP This sauce is a lighter alternative. Use the same amount of chestnut mushrooms, but 200ml (7 fl oz) crème fraîche instead of the double cream. Cook the mushrooms in a saucepan over a high heat for 1 minute in the juice of ½ lemon. Whisk together 1 level dessertspoon cornflour with a little of the crème fraîche in a small bowl (this stabilises and thickens the crème fraîche when heated). Place the remaining crème fraîche in a saucepan and mix in the cornflour mixture. Bring to the boil, whisking all the time. When the sauce has thickened, and just boiled, stir in the mushrooms and lemon juice and allow to cool completely. Spread over the salmon as above and sprinkle with the same topping.

DOUBLE HADDOCK AND HERB FISH CAKES

I'm suggesting that these fish cakes are oven baked, but if preferred they may be fried in butter and oil until crisp and brown.

450g (1 lb) potatoes, peeled
salt and freshly ground
   black pepper
225g (8 oz) undyed smoked
   haddock fillet
225g (8 oz) fresh haddock fillet
a good 25g (1 oz) butter
3 heaped tablespoons
   chopped fresh parsley
1 heaped tablespoon chopped
   fresh dill
2 good tablespoons mayonnaise
a few drops of Tabasco sauce
   to taste
fresh white breadcrumbs

LIGHTER HERB SAUCE
4 tablespoons chopped
   fresh parsley
2 tablespoons chopped fresh dill
4 tablespoons low-fat
   crème fraîche
4 tablespoons 'light'
   low-calorie mayonnaise
4 spring onions, finely sliced
1 tablespoon capers, drained
   and chopped
juice of ½ lemon
salt and freshly ground
   black pepper
a little caster sugar

Preheat the oven to 200°C/Fan 180°C/Gas 6.

STEP 1 Cut the potatoes into even-sized pieces and cook in boiling salted water until tender. Drain well.

STEP 2 Season the fish with salt and pepper and cut the fillets in half if large. Wrap the fish in a foil parcel with the butter. Bake in the preheated oven for 12–15 minutes until the fish is opaque and flakes easily.

STEP 3 Mash the potato with the buttery juices from the cooked fish. Skin the fish, discarding any bones, and flake into a bowl with the mashed potato. Add the herbs, mayonnaise and Tabasco and season well with salt and pepper.

STEP 4 Divide into 12 even-sized round fish cakes. Roll the fish cakes in the breadcrumbs. Cover and chill if time allows.

STEP 5 For the sauce, mix all of the ingredients together. Season, adding a dash of sugar.

STEP 6 Preheat a large baking sheet in the oven with the temperature increased to 220°C/Fan 200°C/Gas 7. Lightly grease a baking sheet with butter and arrange the fish cakes on it in a single layer. Brush with melted butter and bake for 20–25 minutes until crisp, golden and hot through.

STEP 7 Serve with the herb sauce and lemon or lime wedges.

AGA To cook the fish, put the fish parcel in a roasting tin and bake on the lowest set of runners in the Roasting Oven for 10–12 minutes or until the fish is opaque and flakes in the centre when tested with a fork. To cook the fish cakes, preheat a baking sheet or large roasting tin on the floor of the Roasting Oven for 5 minutes, and brush generously with butter. Bake the fish cakes on the sheet or tin for 4 minutes on the floor of the Roasting Oven, turn over and bake for a further 4 minutes until golden brown and piping hot. If need be, they can be kept warm for up to 40 minutes, covered, in the Simmering Oven.

PREPARING AHEAD Prepare the fish cakes to the end of step 4. Cover and store in the fridge for up to 24 hours. Make the sauce on the day. The cakes can be frozen: open-freeze at the end of step 4 until solid, then transfer to a freezer bag and freeze for up to 4 months.

SALMON EN CROÛTE

Salmon en Croûte always makes a lovely festive centrepiece at Christmas. Decorated with puff pastry stars, this recipe is quite simply stunning and relatively quick to make. Any leftovers can be reheated the next day or would be equally delicious served cold.

4 red peppers or 1 x 280g (10 oz) jar roasted mixed peppers in oil
25g (1 oz) butter
225g (8 oz) fresh spinach, washed and coarsely shredded
salt and freshly ground black pepper
1 × 375g (13 oz) packet ready-rolled puff pastry
2 × 700g (1 lb 9 oz) pieces salmon fillet, skinned
1 egg, beaten

SAUCE
300ml (½ pint) double cream
juice of ½ lemon
2 tablespoons green pesto
2 tablespoons chopped fresh basil

Preheat the oven to 220ºC/Fan 200ºC/Gas 7.

STEP 1 If using fresh peppers, cut in half, remove the seeds and place cut-side down on a baking sheet. Slide into the preheated oven and cook for about 30 minutes until charred and soft. Transfer to an oiled bowl, cover tightly with clingfilm (or put in a sealed polythene bag) and leave until cool enough to handle. Remove the skin from the peppers and cut the flesh into thick strips. If using peppers from a jar, drain well and cut into thick strips.

STEP 2 Melt the butter in a large pan, add the shredded spinach and cook quickly until just wilted. Season with salt and pepper and leave to cool. Squeeze out excess moisture. Preheat a large baking tray in the oven.

STEP 3 Roll out half of the pastry really thinly to about 20 × 38cm (8 × 5 in), ideally on non-stick paper (see Tip). Place one fillet of salmon on to the centre of the pastry, season with salt and pepper, and arrange the peppers and spinach on top. Season the second side of salmon, and place on top so that it mirrors the underneath one. Brush the edge of the pastry with beaten egg.

STEP 4 Roll out the remaining pastry really thinly so that it is slightly larger than the bottom layer of pastry. Carefully lift over the salmon, trim off any excess and seal the edges. Re-roll the remaining pastry trimmings thinly. Cut out pastry stars from the trimmings. Brush the pastry covering the salmon with beaten egg, and decorate with the stars. Brush the stars with beaten egg.

Recipe continued overleaf

Recipe continued

STEP 5 Carefully lift on to the preheated baking tray on the non-stick paper, using 2 fish slices, and bake for 30–40 minutes until golden brown. Allow to rest for about 10 minutes while making the sauce.

STEP 6 To make the sauce, heat the cream, add the lemon juice and pesto, and season with salt and pepper. Add the basil just before serving.

STEP 7 Serve the salmon hot in slices with the hot sauce.

AGA Cook on the grid shelf on the floor of the Roasting Oven for about 20 minutes; remove the grid shelf and cook directly on the floor for a further 20 minutes or until golden brown.

PREPARING AHEAD Prepare the salmon to the end of step 4. Wrap in clingfilm and keep in the fridge for up to 24 hours. Remember to preheat the baking tray before cooking the salmon. You could also freeze the salmon in pastry raw, wrapped in foil, then put in a polythene bag and sealed. Thaw for about 18 hours in the fridge.

TIP Non-stick paper is ideal for rolling pastry out on, then transferring the paper and pastry to a baking sheet, then into the oven.

SMOKED HADDOCK FLORENTINE

This very easy version of a fish pie is made in a large dish, perfect for Christmas Eve or a crowd. Ideally assemble the pie the day before. Coating the haddock in cornflour prevents the sauce from becoming too wet. You could serve the pie with rice or mashed potato, but more often than not I just serve garlic or herb bread.

a generous knob of butter
450g (1 lb) button mushrooms, thickly sliced
700g (1½ lb) fresh young spinach
salt and freshly ground black pepper
freshly grated nutmeg
6 hard-boiled eggs, shelled and sliced
1.1kg (2½ lb) undyed smoked haddock fillet, skinned and coated in about 40g (1½ oz) seasoned cornflour
40g (1½ oz) fresh breadcrumbs
75g (3 oz) Parmesan, freshly grated

BÉCHAMEL SAUCE
1.2 litres (2 pints) milk
1 onion, halved
1 bay leaf
a few parsley stalks
100g (4 oz) butter
100g (4 oz) plain flour
100g (4 oz) mature Cheddar, grated
2 teaspoons Dijon mustard

Preheat the oven to 220°C/Fan 200°C/Gas 7.

STEP 1 Measure the milk for the sauce into a saucepan, and add the onion halves, bay leaf and parsley stalks. Bring to just under boiling point, cover and simmer over a low heat for about 30 minutes to flavour the milk. Season with salt and pepper.

STEP 2 Melt the butter for the sauce in a roomy pan, then pull the pan aside from the heat and stir in the flour. Gradually add the strained infused hot milk, return the pan to the heat and slowly bring to the boil, stirring continuously until thickened. Cover the pan with a lid to prevent a skin forming.

STEP 3 Melt the knob of butter in a large, deep frying pan and fry the mushrooms briskly for a minute or so. Add the spinach to the mushrooms and cook gently until it has just wilted. Drain the spinach and mushrooms and season well with salt, pepper and nutmeg.

STEP 4 Mix 6 tablespoons of the béchamel sauce with the spinach and mushrooms and spread on the base of a shallow, buttered ovenproof dish, about 38 × 30cm (15 ×12 in). Cover the spinach and mushrooms with sliced hard-boiled eggs.

Recipe continued overleaf

Recipe continued

STEP 5 Cut the haddock into manageable-sized pieces to give two small pieces per person. Sit these pieces on top of the eggs.

STEP 6 Add the grated Cheddar and Dijon mustard to the remaining sauce and pour over the raw fish. Sprinkle the top with mixed breadcrumbs and Parmesan.

STEP 7 Bake in the preheated oven for about 35 minutes until the haddock is cooked and the topping is golden brown.

AGA Start infusing the milk on the Boiling Plate, then cover and transfer to the Simmering Oven for about 30 minutes. Cook the béchamel sauce on the Simmering Plate. Bake the assembled dish for about 30 minutes on the second set of runners in the Roasting Oven.

PREPARING AHEAD Complete to the end of step 6, cover with clingfilm and keep in the fridge for up to 24 hours.

TIP For Aga fans primarily! I defrost the fish my son often catches by leaving them in their polythene wrapping, covered with an old towel, and putting them in a dish in the Simmering Oven.

FAST-LANE SALMON

A very speedy and stylish fish recipe, which is ideal for large numbers as no last-minute attention is needed. When heating the sauce in the pan, bubble until a good sauce consistency, then add the cucumber and spring onion just before serving, otherwise the sauce will be too runny.

½ × 375g packet ready-rolled puff pastry
4 × 150g (5 oz) centre-cut salmon fillets, skinned
salt and freshly ground black pepper
1 × 200ml (7 fl oz) carton full-fat crème fraîche
50g (2 oz) Parmesan, freshly grated
2 tablespoons chopped fresh parsley
1 egg, beaten
¼ cucumber, peeled, deseeded and chopped to the size of a pine nut
2 spring onions, finely chopped

Preheat the oven to 200ºC/Fan 180ºC/Gas 6.

STEP 1 Roll out the pastry very thinly, and cut into four oblong shapes, each about 7.5 × 15cm (3 × 6 in).

STEP 2 Season the salmon fillets with salt and pepper.

STEP 3 Mix the crème fraîche with half the Parmesan and some salt and pepper. Spread a teaspoon of crème fraîche on to the centre of each fillet, and sprinkle with a tiny amount of chopped parsley.

STEP 4 Wrap a strip of puff pastry around each fillet, over the crème fraîche mixture, ensuring the join is underneath. Arrange on a baking sheet. Lightly score the pastry in a lattice pattern and brush with a little beaten egg. Sprinkle with the remaining Parmesan.

STEP 5 Bake the parcels in the preheated oven for 12–15 minutes until the pastry is crisp and the salmon is cooked right through.

STEP 6 To make the sauce, heat the remaining crème fraîche in a small pan until just hot. Just before serving add the cucumber, spring onions and remaining parsley, and season with salt and pepper. Serve hot with the hot salmon.

AGA Cook the salmon parcels on a baking sheet on the floor of the Roasting Oven for about 8 minutes, then turn the baking sheet round and transfer to the top of the Roasting Oven for about 5 minutes to brown the top.

PREPARING AHEAD The fish can be all prepared and wrapped in pastry, covered in clingfilm and kept in the fridge for up to 24 hours ahead.

TIP This is an easy recipe to double the quantities, or simply freeze the leftover pastry for another time.

AUBERGINE AND GOAT'S CHEESE ROAST

V

A mixture of aubergine, yellow pepper, tomatoes and goat's cheese, with a pesto, cheese and breadcrumb topping. All in one dish, ideal for vegetarians.

2 tablespoons olive oil
2 red onions, sliced into wedges
2 garlic cloves, crushed
2 medium aubergines,
  cut into 2½cm (1 in) chunks
1 yellow pepper, deseeded
  and cut into large dice
2 × 400g (14 oz) cans
  chopped tomatoes
1 tablespoon tomato purée
1½ tablespoons balsamic vinegar
2 teaspoons brown sugar
salt and freshly ground
  black pepper
175g (6 oz) hard goat's
  cheese, cubed
100g (4 oz) breadcrumbs, coarse
2 tablespoons green basil pesto
50g (2 oz) Parmesan, grated

Preheat the oven to 200°C/Fan 180°/Gas 6. You will need a 2 litre (3½ pint) shallow ovenproof dish.

STEP 1 Heat the oil in a large frying pan and cook the onions and garlic over a gentle heat until lightly golden.

STEP 2 Add the aubergines and pepper and fry for about 5 minutes over a high heat until the aubergine chunks are starting to brown and soften.

STEP 3 Add the tomatoes, purée, vinegar and sugar, bring up to the boil, cover with a lid and simmer for 15 minutes. The vegetables should be soft but still hold their shape. Season with salt and pepper and spoon into the dish.

STEP 4 Put the cubes of goat's cheese on top of the vegetable mixture.

STEP 5 Measure the breadcrumbs and pesto into a bowl and rub together using your hands until the crumbs are coated in the pesto. Sprinkle on top of the goat's cheese and spread out to make an even layer. Sprinkle over the Parmesan.

STEP 6 Bake in the oven for about 30 minutes until bubbling around the edges and the crumbs are golden and crispy on top.

STEP 7 Serve with salad and crusty bread.

AGA Cover the vegetables and cook in the Simmering Oven for 20 minutes. Bake the completed dish on the second set of runners in the Roasting Oven for 25 minutes.

PREPARING AHEAD Can be made up to 12 hours ahead in the dish and cooked to serve. Not suitable for freezing.

TIP If you are not keen on goat's cheese you could use another hard cheese like feta or Cheshire.

CHAR-GRILLED VEGETABLE STRUDEL WITH ROQUEFORT

V

You can use any cheese in this recipe, but we like Roquefort best. If you have any leftover cheese from a cheeseboard, e.g. Stilton or mature Cheddar – which is very likely at Christmas time – you can use this as well, but it is important to use a cheese with a strong flavour.

6 sheets filo pastry
50g (2 oz) butter, melted
75g (3 oz) Roquefort
    cheese, sliced

CHAR-GRILLED VEGETABLES
1 onion, sliced into thin wedges
1 yellow pepper, deseeded and
    cut into 2.5cm (1 in) pieces
2 red peppers, deseeded and
    cut into 2.5cm (1 in) pieces
3 courgettes, trimmed and
    sliced into 2.5cm (1 in) pieces
3 tablespoons olive oil
salt and freshly ground
    black pepper

Preheat the oven to 200ºC/Fan 180ºC/Gas 6. Preheat a baking sheet to very hot. Heat a non-stick ridged grill pan or large frying pan until very hot.

STEP 1 Mix the prepared vegetables together with the oil in a polythene bag or bowl, and toss so they are evenly coated. Sprinkle with salt and pepper.

STEP 2 Char-grill the vegetables on the hot grill pan until they are coloured and tender (you may need to do this in batches). Set aside to cool.

STEP 3 Place 2 filo pastry sheets lengthways on a work surface so they are slightly overlapping, to make a rectangle measuring about 35 × 33cm (14 × 13 in). Brush with melted butter, then place another 2 sheets on top widthways, again slightly overlapping. Repeat with another layer, brushing with butter in between.

STEP 4 Spoon half the cooled char-grilled vegetables over the top third of the pastry about 7.5cm (3 in) from the edge and 5cm (2 in) from the sides. Arrange the cheese over the roasted vegetables, and top with the remaining vegetables, so the cheese will be a layer in the middle of the vegetables.

Recipe continued overleaf

Recipe continued

STEP 5 Fold the base and the sides of the pastry in, and roll up to a sausage shape. Brush the strudel with melted butter.

STEP 6 Carefully transfer to the hot baking sheet in the preheated oven, and bake for 20–25 minutes or until golden brown and crisp on top and underneath.

STEP 7 Serve hot in slices with a dressed green salad and garlic bread.

AGA No need to preheat a baking sheet. Slide the strudel on a cold baking sheet directly on to the floor of the Roasting Oven for about 25 minutes or until the pastry is golden and crisp underneath.

PREPARING AHEAD Make the whole strudel first thing in the morning for lunch, or at lunchtime for an evening meal.

TIP This has become one of our firm favourites for lunch – just serve with a dressed salad. Sometimes we use different quantities of the individual vegetables – as long as the total weight is about 1kg (2¼ lb), you can use anything that is in the fridge. If you are using frozen filo, which is inexpensive, always thaw it first, either overnight in the fridge, or at room temperature for about 6 hours. You could substitute 1 small aubergine, cut in half lengthways and sliced, for 1 pepper and 1 courgette. Cook it with the other vegetables.

AUBERGINE FIVE-NUT ROAST

V

This is perfect as a Christmas dinner main course for any vegetarians in the family, and is likely to be devoured by meat eaters too! Any leftovers can be served cold with chutney and salad.

1–2 medium aubergines, sliced thinly lengthways
olive oil
salt and freshly ground black pepper
40g (1½ oz) butter
1 small onion, finely chopped
2 celery sticks, finely chopped
1 garlic clove, crushed
175g (6 oz) shelled mixed nuts (such as Brazils, pine nuts, blanched whole almonds), chopped in the processor, but not too finely
50g (2 oz) shelled pistachio nuts, roughly chopped
100g (4 oz) fresh white breadcrumbs
grated rind and juice of ½ lemon
100g (4 oz) mature Cheddar, grated
100g (4 oz) frozen chestnuts, thawed and roughly chopped
2 eggs, beaten
4 tablespoons chopped fresh parsley

TO SERVE
1 recipe Italian Tomato Sauce (see page 95)

Preheat the grill, and preheat the oven to 200°C/Fan 180°C/Gas 6. Line a 900g (2 lb) loaf tin, 17 × 9 × 9cm (6½ × 3½ × 3½ in) base measurement, with foil and oil lightly.

STEP 1 Arrange the aubergines on a large oiled baking tray in a single layer, brush or drizzle with olive oil and season with salt and pepper. Cook under the hot grill for 5–7 minutes each side, until the aubergine has softened and is beginning to turn golden. The aubergine will cook to a deep brown once in the oven, so don't worry about getting too much colour at this stage. Once you have turned the aubergine slices over, do keep a close eye on them as the second side will colour more quickly than the first. Allow to cool slightly. Use to line across the base and sides of the prepared loaf tin, all slices going in the same direction.

STEP 2 Melt the butter in a medium pan, add the onion, celery and garlic and cook, stirring occasionally, until soft, about 10 minutes. Spoon into a large bowl and leave to cool.

STEP 3 Add the remaining ingredients to the bowl with plenty of seasoning, and stir well to mix.

Recipe continued overleaf

AGA Cook the aubergine slices on a griddle pan, turning over until golden brown. Sit the completed loaf tin in a small roasting tin. Bake on the lowest set of runners in the Roasting Oven for 45–55 minutes until set and piping hot.

PREPARING AHEAD You can prepare the nut roast the day before up to the end of step 4. Keep in the fridge, then cook as directed. Alternatively it can be made and completed up to 2 days ahead. This also freezes very successfully. Turn out of the tin, allow to cool, then wrap and freeze for up to a month.

To reheat, put the nut loaf on to a baking tray and cover with foil. Reheat in the oven preheated to 180°C/Fan 160°C/Gas 4 for 50 minutes to 1 hour or until piping hot throughout.

TIP If you cannot get frozen chestnuts, soak 50g (2 oz) dried chestnuts overnight.

Recipe continued

STEP 4 Spoon into the loaf tin, pressing the mixture down firmly. Fold the ends of aubergine over the top of the filling and cover the tin with foil.

STEP 5 Cook in the preheated oven for 50 minutes to 1 hour. Turn out on to a serving plate, remove the tin and garnish with sprigs of flat-leaf parsley.

STEP 6 Slice thickly and serve with the hot Italian Tomato Sauce.

✦ SERVES 8 ✦

ITALIAN TOMATO SAUCE

V

This sauce is served with the Aubergine Five-nut Roast on page 93, but is also good with pasta too.

2 tablespoons olive oil
1 medium onion, finely chopped
2 garlic cloves, crushed
2 × 500g (1 lb 2 oz) cartons
   tomato passata
2 tablespoons sun-dried
   tomato paste
2 tablespoons red pesto
a little Worcestershire sauce
2 teaspoons caster sugar
salt and freshly ground
   black pepper

STEP 1 Heat the oil in a medium pan and cook the onion and garlic over a gentle heat until soft but not coloured, about 10 minutes.

STEP 2 Add the remaining ingredients to the pan, bring to the boil, then simmer very gently for about 10 minutes. Adjust seasoning to serve.

AGA Fry the onion and garlic in the oil on the Boiling Plate. Add the remaining ingredients, bring to the boil, then transfer to the Simmering Oven for about 20 minutes.

PREPARING AHEAD Make the sauce up to 2 days ahead, pour into a bowl, cool, cover and keep in the fridge until ready to reheat. Reheat in a pan until piping hot. To freeze, cool the sauce, pack into a freezerproof container and freeze for up to 3 months. Thaw overnight and reheat in a pan until piping hot.

TIP I prefer red pesto for this recipe, but if you have only green in the cupboard, then use that instead.

CHRISTMAS ROASTS

CHAPTER FOUR

Birds for roasting reign supreme at Christmas. Goose used to be the prime British celebratory bird until turkey, the new-fangled bird from the Americas, was introduced in the sixteenth century. I have given recipes for both roast goose and turkey here, with many of their traditional accompaniments such as Sausages Wrapped in Bacon, Gravy, Bread and Apple Sauce, and stuffings. Order your turkey or goose well in advance, preferably fresh, and collect it (or best of all, have it delivered) on the 23rd or 24th. You can then get started with some of the preparations: making a stock from the giblets, making the stuffing, and actually stuffing the turkey (neck end only) before storing in the fridge. Look too at the introductory pages for lots of information on planning and preparation.

There are several ideas in the Buffets chapter for using up leftover turkey (you'll rarely have any goose left to eat later), as well as some alternative recipes for chicken and duck if you get tired of turkey (although I rarely do!).

It has become quite common for families to celebrate Christmas with a rib roast of beef instead of the traditional roast bird and so I have included a recipe for that here. It would make a splendid lunch on New Year's Day, too. Its inevitable partner, the Yorkshire Pudding (this is one which can be made ahead), is here, but you'll find the Roast Potatoes, Roast Parsnips, and other vegetables in the following chapter.

TRADITIONAL ROAST TURKEY

I use a meat thermometer when cooking turkey – it helps to judge when the turkey is done. Cook it to 75°–80°C rather than the 90°C suggested on the thermometer gauge. When working out when to put the turkey in the oven, allow at least 30 minutes' resting time. See also my tips in the Introduction (pages 10–11).

1 × 6.3kg (14 lb) oven-ready turkey
about 100g (4 oz) butter, softened
1 lemon, thinly sliced (optional)
3 small sprigs of fresh thyme
  (optional)
½ recipe Lemon and Thyme
  Pork Stuffing (see page 104)
1 onion, cut into wedges

Preheat the oven to 220°C/Fan 200°C/Gas 7.

STEP 1 Loosen the skin over the breast of the turkey by slipping your fingers between the flesh and skin at the neck end, leaving the skin attached at the cavity end. Spread softened butter over the top of the breast under the skin, holding the skin up. Slip the lemon slices and thyme sprigs in under the skin. The latter is a nice addition, but if time is short forget this variation.

STEP 2 Stuff the neck end of the turkey up to the breast with the stuffing. Secure the loose skin with fine skewers, or just tuck the skin underneath. Fill the body cavity with any lemon trimmings, herbs and large pieces of onion. Tie the legs with string to give a neat shape. Lightly butter the skin of the bird.

STEP 3 Calculate the cooking time. If you have chosen to cook a turkey of a different size to above, see chart on page 101. (No need to include the stuffing weight.) Arrange two sheets of foil across a large roasting tin: they must be large enough to go generously up and over the turkey breast. Place the turkey on top and, if using a meat thermometer, insert it into the thickest part of the thigh. (When cooked it will register 75°–80°C.) Fold the sheets of foil loosely over the turkey, leaving a large air gap between the turkey and the foil.

STEP 4 Cook the turkey in the preheated oven for 40 minutes. Reduce the oven temperature to 160°C/Fan 140°C/Gas 3, and continue to roast for 3½ hours, basting from time to time.

Recipe continued overleaf

Recipe continued

STEP 5 Increase the oven heat to 220°C/Fan 200°C/Gas 7 again. Take the turkey out of the oven, turn back the foil and drain off any surplus juices from the tin into a jug or bowl. Leave the fat to rise to the top in a cold place. When the liquid is cold, take off the fat with a spoon and save the juices for the gravy. Baste the bird, and return it to the hot oven for about 30 minutes for the skin to brown and become crisp.

STEP 6 Take the turkey out of the oven and check if cooked. If not using a thermometer, pierce the thickest part of the thigh with a small sharp knife. If the juices are clear, then the turkey is done; if they are still tinged with pink, then roast for a little longer. If the juices are clear cover the bird again with the foil, and leave to stand for 30 minutes before carving.

STEP 7 Serve with Sausages Wrapped in Bacon, giblet gravy, Bread Sauce, Scarlet Confit and Apricot and Chestnut Stuffing (see pages 106, 108, 105, 110 and 112).

PREPARING AHEAD Prepare up to the end of step 3 up to 12 hours before. Cover and chill until ready to cook. The stuffings can of course be made up to a month in advance and frozen.

TIP Do not put a meat stuffing into the cavity of a bird as this is not safe. Put in only flavouring vegetables and herbs.

GAS AND ELECTRIC COOKING CHART

OVEN-READY TURKEY	STARTING TEMPERATURE (FOIL ON)	ROASTING TEMPERATURE (FOIL ON)	BROWNING TEMPERATURE (FOIL OPEN)
	220°C/Fan 200°C/ Gas 7	160°C/Fan 140°C/ Gas 3	220°C/Fan 200°C/ Gas 7
3.5–5kg (8–11 lb)	30 mins	2½–3 hours	about 30 mins
5.4–6.3kg (12–14 lb)	40 mins	3–3½ hours	about 30 mins
6.75–9kg (15–20 lb)	45 mins	3½–4½ hours	about 30 mins

Ovens vary considerably, so if you know that yours is on the hot side or the cool side, adjust the above cooking times.

AGA

AGA SLOW ROASTING

AFTER STEP 3
Place on the floor of the Simmering Oven.

❋ 3.5–4.5kg (8–12 lb) turkey is best fast roasted, see opposite.

❋ 5.4–6.3kg (12–14 lb) turkey, 10–13 hours (overnight)

❋ 6.75–9kg (15–20 lb) turkey, 12–14 hours (overnight)

To brown
When the bird is done, uncover the foil and transfer to the Roasting Oven for about 15 minutes until golden. If the turkey is over 8.1kg (18 lb), or if your Simmering Oven is on the cool side, start off in the Roasting Oven uncovered for 30 minutes, then cover with foil and transfer to the Simmering Oven (see above).

AGA FAST ROASTING

AFTER STEP 3
Cook in the roasting tin lightly covered with foil on the grid shelf on the floor of the Roasting Oven. Baste the bird from time to time. Remove the foil 30 minutes before the end of cooking time to crisp the skin.

❋ 3.6–4.5kg (8–11 lb) turkey, 1¾–2¼ hours

❋ 5.4–6.3kg (12–14 lb) turkey, about 2½ hours

❋ 6.75–9kg (15–20 lb) turkey, about 3 hours

ROAST TURKEY CROWN

Great alternative to roasting a large bird, the crown is the turkey breasts and wing joints with the legs removed.

4–4.5kg (9–10 lb 2 oz) turkey
    crown on the bone
1 lemon, thinly sliced
3 small sprigs of fresh thyme
75g (3 oz) butter, softened

Preheat the oven to 220°C/Fan 200°C/Gas 6.

STEP 1 Line a large roasting tin with foil. Loosen the skin over the breast of the turkey and arrange the lemon and thyme in a neat layer between the skin and breast. Spread with the soft butter.

STEP 2 Put the turkey crown into the roasting tin. Roast in the middle of the oven for 25–30 minutes until lightly golden brown. Reduce the temperature to 180°C/Fan 160°C/Gas 4 and continue to roast for 1½–1¾ hours until golden and cooked through. Test if the bird is cooked by inserting a skewer into the thickest part of the breast and checking that the juices run clear. The temperature of the thickest part of the breast should be about 75°C, if tested with a thermometer.

STEP 3 Leave to rest for 20 minutes before carving.

AGA Roast in the Roasting Oven for about 1¼ hours or until cooked. If getting too brown cover the breast with foil.

PREPARING AHEAD Can be roasted up to 2 days ahead to serve cold.

LEMON AND THYME PORK STUFFING

This is a favourite family recipe, served for every Christmas as long as I can remember! This is the stuffing for the neck end of the turkey: do not put a meat stuffing in the body cavity of a bird.

25g (1 oz) butter
1 small onion, chopped
450g (1 lb) pork sausagemeat
50g (2 oz) fresh white
   breadcrumbs
finely grated zest and juice
   of ½ large lemon
salt and freshly ground
   black pepper
2 tablespoons chopped
   fresh parsley
leaves from 3 sprigs
   of fresh thyme

STEP 1 Melt the butter in a saucepan, add the onion and cook gently until soft, about 10 minutes.

STEP 2 Stir in the remaining ingredients and mix well together. Cool before stuffing the turkey.

STEP 3 This is now ready to stuff the neck end of the bird.

AGA Cook the onion, covered, in the Simmering Oven for about 15 minutes until soft.

PREPARING AHEAD Make the day before, cover and keep in the fridge. Use to stuff the neck end of the bird the day before roasting, providing the bird will fit in the fridge. The stuffing can also be made and frozen for up to a month in advance.

TIP Breadcrumbs are often used in recipes over Christmas. Some time in advance, whiz a whole loaf to breadcrumbs in the processor and keep in the freezer. You will then have them at the ready, and they defrost in minutes. This amount is sufficient to stuff a 7.2–8.1kg (16–18 lb) turkey in the neck end.

BREAD SAUCE

In recent years I have been freezing bread sauce, and am surprised that it freezes so well. Just one less job to do on Christmas Day…

1 onion, quartered
4 cloves
2 bay leaves
450ml (¾ pint) milk
100g (4 oz) fresh white
    breadcrumbs
150ml (¼ pint) double cream
25g (1 oz) butter
salt and freshly ground
    black pepper
a little freshly grated nutmeg

STEP 1 Stud each peeled onion quarter with a clove, and put into a pan with the bay leaves and the milk. Bring to the boil, take the pan off the heat, cover and leave to infuse for about10 minutes.

STEP 2 Lift the onion and bay leaves out of the milk with a slotted spoon and discard. Add the breadcrumbs to the pan, and bring to the boil, stirring. Simmer for 1–2 minutes.

STEP 3 Stir in the cream and butter, then add salt, pepper and freshly grated nutmeg to taste. Serve hot.

AGA To infuse the milk, bring to the boil with the onion, cloves and bay leaves, cover and transfer to the Simmering Oven for 15 minutes. Complete the bread sauce on the Simmering Plate on the day.

PREPARING AHEAD Unless frozen, bread sauce is best made on the day, otherwise it tends to turn grey. Freeze for up to 1 month. Thaw overnight at room temperature. To reheat the bread sauce, spoon into a small pan and gradually whisk in a little milk until smooth and the required consistency. Reheat gently.

TIP To be really well organised, freeze bread crust crumbs and bread non-crust crumbs separately. The crust crumbs are good for stuffings; the breadcrumbs can be used in bread sauce and as the topping for a gratin.

SAUSAGES WRAPPED IN BACON

Cocktail sausages from the supermarket rather than from the butcher tend to come in packs of 18. Double up the recipe if you want more – they're always a hit with children! Try to buy a good-quality smoked or unsmoked streaky bacon rather than one which is thin and full of water – it makes all the difference.

6 long slices dry-cured
    streaky bacon
18 cocktail sausages

Preheat the oven to 190ºC/Fan 170ºC/Gas 5.

STEP 1 Stretch each bacon rasher with the back of a knife and cut each rasher into three.

STEP 2 Wrap a piece of bacon tightly around each sausage, and put on to a baking tray ready for cooking.

STEP 3 Cook in the preheated oven for about 45 minutes or until cooked and crisp. Serve hot with the roast turkey.

AGA Arrange the sausages on a grill rack in the roasting tin. Slide on to the top set of runners in the Roasting Oven, and cook for about 20 minutes, turning halfway through.

PREPARING AHEAD Prepare up to the end of step 2. Cover and keep in the fridge. You could also freeze the wrapped sausages at the end of step 2. Thaw overnight in the fridge and cook as directed.

GIBLET STOCK

Make this with the giblets of a turkey or goose. If you like a richer stock, roast the giblets in a roasting tin in a preheated oven 200ºC/Fan 180ºC/Gas 6 for about 15 minutes or until lightly brown before adding the water (step 1).

giblets from the bird (neck, heart
 and gizzard, but not the liver)
1 onion, unpeeled and quartered
1 celery stick, roughly chopped
1 large carrot, roughly chopped
parsley stalks
6 black peppercorns

STEP 1 Put the giblets into a large pan. Add 1 litre (1¾ pints) water and bring to the boil, skimming off any scum that forms on the surface.

STEP 2 Add the remaining ingredients, cover and simmer for about 1 hour. Strain the stock, cool, cover and keep in the fridge before using for gravy.

AGA Bring the stock to the boil on the Boiling Plate, cover then transfer to the Simmering Oven for about 3 hours.

PREPARING AHEAD Prepare up to a day ahead, cool quickly, cover and keep in the fridge.

TIP The liver from a turkey or goose makes a wonderful pâté.

CHRISTMAS TURKEY GRAVY

The gravy is a very important part of the Christmas meal, so you should use a good stock made from the giblets for the best flavour. If you haven't any port, use red wine instead.

25g (1 oz) plain flour
600ml (1 pint) Giblet Stock
    (see opposite)
150ml (¼ pint) port
2 tablespoons redcurrant jelly
salt and freshly ground
    black pepper

STEP 1 Pour off the turkey juices into a bowl or jug. Spoon off 2 tablespoons of the turkey fat (which will be floating at the top) into the same unwashed roasting tin. Spoon off the remaining fat from the juices and discard.

STEP 2 Put the tin over a medium heat and add the flour. Cook for about 1 minute, stirring well to scrape any sediment from the tin. Gradually pour in the stock and port, and whisk well. Add the redcurrant jelly, bring to the boil, then simmer for 2–3 minutes.

STEP 3 Add the skimmed juices from the roast turkey and adjust the seasoning. Strain into a warmed gravy boat to serve.

PREPARING AHEAD Make the gravy the day before, using 2 tablespoons vegetable oil instead of the turkey fat. On the day, drain the fat from the roasting tin, add the gravy to the sediment in the tin and bring to the boil. Strain before serving.

TIP Some families like a huge amount of gravy. If so, double this recipe. Any left over can be added to a soup made from the turkey bones (see page 71).

SCARLET CONFIT

V

This is my version of cranberry sauce – it is perfect with roast turkey or game.

450g (1 lb) fresh or frozen
   cranberries
225g (8 oz) granulated sugar
finely grated zest and juice
   of 1 orange
50ml (2 fl oz) port
50ml (2 fl oz) cider vinegar
a large pinch of ground allspice
a large pinch of ground cinnamon

STEP 1 Measure all the ingredients into a shallow saucepan.

STEP 2 Bring to the boil and simmer gently for 10–15 minutes, stirring from time to time. Don't worry if it looks a bit runny as it thickens when it cools.

STEP 3 Serve warm or cold.

AGA Cook uncovered in the Simmering Oven for about 1 hour.

PREPARING AHEAD Cook and keep covered in the fridge for up to 3 weeks. You could freeze it too, for up to 3 months.

APRICOT AND CHESTNUT STUFFING

V

This stuffing is cooked in a separate dish rather than inside the bird, so it becomes very crisp. It is really good with turkey, goose or chicken.

225g (8 oz) ready-to-eat
   dried apricots
1 large onion, coarsely chopped
225g (8 oz) fresh white
   breadcrumbs
75g (3 oz) butter, plus extra
   for greasing
225g (8 oz) frozen chestnuts,
   thawed and roughly chopped
a generous bunch of fresh
   parsley, chopped
salt and freshly ground
   black pepper

Preheat the oven to 190ºC/Fan 170ºC/Gas 5. You will need a shallow ovenproof dish, about 20 × 28 x 5cm (8 × 11 x 2 in).

STEP 1 Chop the apricots into small pieces the size of raisins.

STEP 2 Measure 600ml (1 pint) water into a pan, add the onion and apricot pieces, and boil for 5 minutes. Drain well.

STEP 3 Put the breadcrumbs into a large bowl. Melt the measured butter in a non-stick frying pan, and pour half of it on to the breadcrumbs.

STEP 4 Add the chestnuts to the remaining melted butter in the frying pan and brown lightly. Mix together with the apricots, onion, parsley and breadcrumbs. Season well with salt and pepper.

STEP 5 Turn into a buttered ovenproof dish and bake in the preheated oven for about 30 minutes until crisp.

AGA Slide the dish on to the floor of the Roasting Oven for 25–30 minutes until crisp.

PREPARING AHEAD Prepare to the end of step 4. Cover and keep in the fridge for up to 24 hours before cooking. Cook as above but for a little longer. If preferred, cook the day before and reheat until piping hot on the day. You could also freeze it at the end of step 4, for about 1 month.

TIP Buy frozen chestnuts as soon as you see them in the supermarkets (mid November), as they sell out very quickly!

SAGE AND ONION STUFFING

This is a really good recipe for sage and onion stuffing which I have been making for years. It's wonderful with roast goose (see page 114). I prefer to cook and serve it in a separate dish (rather than in the bird itself), which makes it wonderfully golden and crisp.

450g (1 lb) onions,
roughly chopped
300ml (½ pint) water
75g (3 oz) butter, plus
extra for greasing
1 tablespoon fresh sage,
finely chopped
225g (8 oz) fresh white
breadcrumbs
salt and freshly ground
black pepper

STEP 1 Put the onions and water in a pan, bring to the boil and simmer for 15 minutes. Drain well.

STEP 2 Stir the remaining ingredients into the pan and mix well. Allow to cool completely if you are going to use it to stuff the neck of the goose or turkey.

Preheat the oven to 190°C/Fan 170°C/Gas 5.

STEP 3 To cook the stuffing separately, which I much prefer, spoon the mixture into a shallow, buttered ovenproof dish and bake in the preheated oven for 25–30 minutes until golden and crisp.

AGA Cook on the floor of the Roasting Oven for about 15 minutes or until the top is golden brown and crisp. Reheat on the grid shelf near the top of the Roasting Oven for about 10 minutes.

PREPARING AHEAD Prepare the stuffing the day before. Cover and keep in the fridge. Cook as directed. Or, you can cook the stuffing in a dish, cool, keep in the fridge overnight and reheat the following day. The prepared stuffing can be frozen. Thaw overnight at cool room temperature and cook as directed. Or, freeze the baked stuffing in its dish, thaw overnight at cool room temperature and reheat as directed.

ROAST GOOSE

Traditionally, goose used to be the favoured bird to roast at Christmas rather than turkey. Turkey certainly offers more scope for eating up on Boxing Day, but for a small family gathering a roast goose is a treat not to be missed. It has a very special flavour. As with turkey, you may need to order a fresh goose in advance.

1 × 4.5–5.5kg (10–12 lb) oven-ready goose, with giblets reserved for stock
apple peelings (reserved from making the apple sauce), lemon rind and sprigs of sage etc. for the cavity
salt and freshly ground black pepper

GRAVY
25g (1 oz) plain flour
600ml (1 pint) Giblet Stock (see page 108)

Preheat the oven to 220ºC/Fan 200ºC/Gas 7.

STEP 1 To remove feather stubs from the skin of the goose, use the tip of a sharp knife or tweezers. Pull any surplus fat from the cavity of the goose and put the apple peelings, lemon rind and sprigs of sage into the cavity. Season with salt and pepper and rub the outside of the goose with more seasoning.

STEP 2 Place the goose, breast-side down, on a wire rack set in a large roasting tin and roast in the preheated oven for about 30 minutes until brown.

STEP 3 Turn the goose so that it is breast-side up, and cook for a further 20 minutes until the breast skin is brown. Pour the fat from the roasting tin into a heatproof bowl and save for roasting the potatoes. (The easiest way to do this is to lift the rack and goose on to a board, then pour the fat from the tin into a bowl. Also check once or twice during the remaining cooking time to see if any more needs pouring off.)

STEP 4 Reduce the oven temperature to 180ºC/Fan 160ºC/Gas 4, and cook for a further 1½–2 hours or until the goose is cooked. Test the goose by inserting a fine skewer into the thickest part of the thigh – the juices should run clear when the goose is cooked.

Recipe continued overleaf

Recipe continued

STEP 5 Lift the cooked goose on to a serving board or platter, tightly cover with foil and leave to rest for about 20 minutes.

STEP 6 Make the gravy while the goose is resting. Pour off all but 2 tablespoons of fat from the roasting tin, put the tin over a medium heat and add the flour. Cook for about 1 minute, stirring well to scrape any sediment from the tin. Gradually pour in the stock, whisk well, bring to the boil, then simmer for 2–3 minutes or until the required consistency. Season to taste and strain into a warmed gravy boat to serve.

STEP 7 Serve the goose with Apple Sauce and Sage and Onion Stuffing (see pages 117 and 113). Braised Red Cabbage (see page 136) goes particularly well with roast goose.

AGA At step 2, roast the goose on the lowest set of runners in the Roasting Oven for about 30 minutes until brown, turn over and roast the breast side until golden. Transfer to the Simmering Oven for about 3 hours until tender. Just before serving, re-crisp the skin in the tin on the lowest set of runners in the Roasting Oven for about 10 minutes.

PREPARING AHEAD The goose can be prepared for the oven the day before, to the end of step 1 (without the seasoning). Cover loosely and keep in the fridge, and season before roasting.

TIP Goose fat is excellent for roasting potatoes. Store excess in the fridge for up to 2 months.

APPLE SAUCE

V

Apple sauce complements goose perfectly. It needs to be sharp to counteract the richness of the goose, so don't add too much sugar – about 3 tablespoons should do.

900g (2 lb) cooking apples
juice of 1 lemon
50g (2 oz) butter
caster sugar to taste

STEP 1 Peel, core and slice the apples (reserve the apple peelings to put in the cavity of the goose, if that's what the sauce is for). Put the apple slices in a pan with 3 tablespoons water and the lemon juice. Cover and cook gently until the apples are soft, stirring occasionally.

STEP 2 Beat the soft apples well with a wooden spoon and add the butter and sugar to taste. Serve hot.

AGA Cook the apple sauce gently on the Simmering Plate, or bring to the boil, then transfer to the Simmering Oven and cook until the apples are soft, stirring occasionally.

PREPARING AHEAD Make the day before, cool, cover and store in the fridge. Reheat in a pan, stirring. To freeze, cool the sauce, spoon into a freezerproof container and freeze for up to 3 months. Thaw overnight, put into a pan and reheat over a gentle heat, stirring.

TIP If you like a chunkier apple sauce, just mash the cooked apple rather than beating it.

ROAST FILLET OF PORK WITH CRANBERRY AND MADEIRA GRAVY

For a roast, this impressive dish is easy to do. It is a fast recipe as it can be assembled ahead, then roasted on the day. It also carves easily, as there are no bones to fuss about. It is two pork fillets, flattened out, then filled with a herbed mushroom stuffing and wrapped in bacon. It has the 'wow' factor and would make an original alternative to a roast bird at Christmas.

2 pork fillets of equal length, each about 450g (1 lb) in weight, trimmed of all fat
10–12 long streaky bacon rashers
salt and freshly ground black pepper

STUFFING
1 tablespoon sunflower oil
1 medium onion, finely chopped
225g (8 oz) chestnut mushrooms, chopped
40g (1½ oz) Parmesan, freshly grated
25g (1 oz) fresh white breadcrumbs
3–4 tablespoons chopped fresh parsley
1 teaspoon chopped fresh thyme leaves
1 egg yolk

CRANBERRY AND MADEIRA GRAVY
25g (1 oz) butter
100g (4 oz) chestnut mushrooms, sliced
300ml (½ pint) cranberry juice
75ml (2½ fl oz) Madeira
1 rounded tablespoon plain flour
1 tablespoon balsamic vinegar

Preheat the oven to 220°C/Fan 200°C/Gas 7.

STEP 1 First make the stuffing. Heat the oil in a frying pan, add the onion and fry for a few minutes over a low heat until tender. Add the chopped mushrooms to the onion, and cook over a high heat to drive off any liquid from the mushrooms. When the pan is completely dry, take off the heat and add all the remaining stuffing ingredients, seasoning with salt and pepper. Set aside to cool.

STEP 2 Split the pork fillets lengthways halfway through (but not entirely in half), open out and cover with clingfilm. Using a rolling pin, beat out to flat. Stretch the bacon rashers with the back of a knife, and arrange overlapping on a chopping board.

STEP 3 Put one of the fillets on to the bacon, season with black pepper and spread with the stuffing. Cover with the other fillet, beaten side facing down. Roll up tightly, folding each piece of bacon over the roll. Lift into a roasting tin with the bacon join underneath.

STEP 4 Bake in the preheated oven for about an hour until the bacon is crisp and the pork is cooked.

Recipe continued overleaf

Recipe continued

STEP 5 While the pork is roasting, make the gravy. Melt the butter in a saucepan, add the sliced mushrooms, and cook for a few minutes. Gradually pour in the cranberry juice. In a small bowl blend the Madeira with the flour until smooth, then add to the sauce. Bring to the boil, stirring, then add the balsamic vinegar. Season with salt and pepper.

STEP 6 Allow the pork to rest for a minimum of 10 minutes. Add the roasting tin juices to the gravy if they are not too salty.

STEP 7 Carve the pork, and serve with the gravy and some mashed potato.

AGA Cook at the top of the Roasting Oven for about an hour until tender and brown.

PREPARING AHEAD Prepare the fillets a day ahead, and roast to serve.

TIP This freezes well raw, then you can thaw in the fridge. Some juices will come out on thawing. These can be added to the gravy.

⤃ SERVES 8 ⤄

THE BEST
YORKSHIRE PUDDING

This is an essential accompaniment to roast beef. Use a ladle to divide the batter between the individual tins, or pour the mixture from a jug.

100g (4 oz) plain flour
a pinch of salt
3 eggs, beaten
225ml (8 fl oz) milk
white vegetable fat for greasing

Preheat the oven to 220ºC/Fan 200ºC/Gas 7.

STEP 1 Measure the flour into a bowl with the salt. Make a well in the flour and add the eggs and a little milk. Whisk the eggs and milk together, taking a little flour from the sides, then whisk in the remaining milk gradually, drawing in all of the flour to make a smooth batter.

STEP 2 Generously grease two sets of four-hole Yorkshire pudding tins or a 30 × 23cm (12 × 9 in) roasting tin with white vegetable fat. Heat the fat in the tins in the preheated oven.

STEP 3 When the fat is sizzling hot, pour the batter into the prepared individual tins or into the roasting tin. Cook the individual puddings for 15–20 minutes and the large pudding for 25–30 minutes or until well risen and a good brown colour.

AGA Cook on the lowest set of runners in the Roasting Oven for about 20 minutes for the large Yorkshire and 15 minutes for the individual ones. If making the Yorkshire pudding ahead, reheat in the Roasting Oven for about 7 minutes or until just crisp and hot.

PREPARING AHEAD Yorkshire pudding reheats extremely well. Cook the day before, leave in the tins and allow to cool. Keep in a cool place overnight. Reheat in the oven, preheated to 200°C/Fan 180°C/Gas 6 for 10–15 minutes for the small puddings and 15–20 minutes for the large pudding. You can also freeze Yorkshire puddings. Cool, then pack and freeze for up to 2 months. Cook from frozen at 200ºC/Fan 180ºC/Gas 6 for about 20 minutes for the small puddings and 25 minutes for the large pudding.

TIP There is no need to leave batter to stand and rest, as long as the batter is smooth.

ROAST PRIME RIB OF BEEF

Something very special. Prime rib (fore rib) and wing rib are first-class roasting cuts of meat. Serve with the usual accompaniments – Yorkshire Pudding, Roast Potatoes and horseradish sauce (see pages 121, 131 and 227) – or you could try the Beetroot and Horseradish on page 139.

1 × 2-rib joint, either prime rib cut short, or wing rib cut short, about 2.3kg (5 lb)
salt and freshly ground black pepper
1 large onion, unpeeled but thickly sliced

GOOD GRAVY
3 tablespoons dripping
1 good tablespoon plain flour
75ml (2½ fl oz) port
500ml (18 fl oz) beef stock
a dash of Worcestershire sauce
a little gravy browning

Preheat the oven to 220°C/Fan 200°C/Gas 7.

STEP 1 Sprinkle the beef fat with salt and pepper. Stand on end in a roasting tin just large enough for the joint on a bed of thick slices of unpeeled onion (the onion skin gives colour to the juices). If using a meat thermometer, insert into the meat in the thickest part. Transfer to the centre of the preheated oven for 15 minutes, then lower the temperature to 180°C/Fan 160°C/Gas 4. Roast as per the chart below, basting from time to time.

STEP 2 When the meat is done, check the thermometer and see chart below. Lift out of the tin, loosely cover with foil and leave to rest in a warm place for about 20 minutes before carving. Discard the onion, squeezing any juices into the tin.

STEP 3 Meanwhile, make the gravy. Skim off 3 good tablespoons of fat from the roasting tin. Pour the juices into a bowl and put in the fridge for the fat to rise to the top. Measure the flour into the tin, and whisk with the 3 reserved tablespoons of fat over the heat. Gradually add the port and stock, then the Worcestershire sauce. Remove the fat from the bowl of juices in the fridge, and add the juices to the gravy, along with a little gravy browning. Check the seasoning.

STEP 4 To carve, slip a sharp knife close to the bone to free the complete joint, then carve down across the grain.

ROASTING CHART

BEEF	OVEN TEMPERATURE	TIME	INTERNAL TEMP
Rare	180°C/Fan160°C/Gas 4	15 mins per 450g (1 lb)	60°C
Medium	180°C/Fan160°C/Gas 4	20 mins per 450g (1 lb)	70°C
Well-done	180°C/Fan160°C/Gas 4	25 mins per 450g (1 lb)	75°C

Individual ovens do vary, and these times are only a guide. A meat thermometer is the best way to ensure a properly cooked roast. I preheat the oven to 220°C/Fan 200°C/Gas 7 and roast for 15 minutes, then follow the chart here.

AGA Roast the beef in the Roasting Oven with a meat thermometer following the chart above.

VEGETABLES
AND SIDES

CHAPTER FIVE

Most of the vegetables here are for vegetable accompaniments for fish, meat, poultry and game dishes. You'll find some good ideas for potatoes – particularly my Roast Potatoes, vital for the turkey or roast beef – and some interesting ways of cooking the winter root vegetables which are so much part of our diet at this time of year. I have chosen a selection of other dishes that are perfect, to my mind, with Christmas roasts, notably the Braised Red Cabbage and Buttered Brussels Sprouts.

We always think of vegetable cooking as a last-minute job, but many of the recipes here can be prepared ahead of time. You could part-cook roasted vegetables (usually root) until golden the day before, then all you have to do on the day is blast them in a very hot oven to get them brown and crisp. This is particularly handy with Christmas Day roast potatoes! Root vegetable purées are a favourite of mine, one of which I give here, and they can be fully made at least the day before.

BUTTERED BRUSSELS SPROUTS

V

Sprouts are an essential part of Christmas lunch, although not everyone likes them! The debate will run and run as to whether a cross should be cut in the base of the sprout or not – you choose! This is one vegetable that really can't be kept hot. Cooking and serving the sprouts should be the last job before you sit down to eat.

900g (2 lb) Brussels sprouts
about 25g (1 oz) butter
salt and freshly ground
    black pepper

STEP 1 Prepare the sprouts, removing the outer leaves. Trim the base, and cut a cross in the base of each sprout if you wish.

STEP 2 Cook in boiling salted water for 5–6 minutes, depending on size, until just cooked – don't overcook!

STEP 3 Drain, toss in the butter, season and serve immediately.

VARIATIONS
Once boiled, stir-fry the sprouts with lardons of bacon until the bacon is crisp.

Halve the boiled sprouts and stir-fry with sliced leeks.

Toss the sprouts in butter with chopped herbs such as chives and parsley.

Serve boiled sprouts with toasted almonds or chopped chestnuts.

Serve boiled sprouts with grated orange zest.

AGA Cook on the Boiling Plate. Continue with step 3.

PREPARING AHEAD Prepare the sprouts the day before, put into a polythene bag and keep in the fridge. Don't keep them in water – it is not necessary.

✦ **SERVES 8** ✦

ROAST PARSNIPS

If you want to prepare ahead, then blanch the parsnips the day before and half-roast them if you wish (see below). But you must blanch them if you peel and prepare them, or they will turn brown. If you are really pushed for time and haven't blanched the parsnips, then they can be roasted without blanching – they will simply take a little longer.

900g (2 lb) parsnips, peeled
salt and freshly ground
   black pepper
about 2 tablespoons goose fat

Preheat the oven to 220°C/Fan 200°C/Gas 7.

STEP 1 Cut the parsnips into chunky lengths. Add to a pan of boiling salted water and cook for about 3 minutes. Drain well.

STEP 2 Heat the goose fat in a large roasting tin in the preheated oven. When sizzling hot, add the parsnips, spoon over the fat to evenly coat and roast until golden, 20–25 minutes, depending on size. Turn the parsnips over in the fat and roast for a further 15–20 minutes until a deep gold.

STEP 3 Season with salt and freshly ground black pepper to serve.

AGA Heat the goose fat in the roasting tin on the floor of the Roasting Oven until sizzling. Add the parsnips and continue to cook on the floor of the Roasting Oven for 30–40 minutes.

PREPARING AHEAD Blanch the parsnips the day before if you wish. Cool, cover and keep in a cool place overnight. You can also half-roast the parsnips the day before. Roast until a pale golden, 20–25 minutes depending on size, remove from the fat and cool. On Christmas Day, re-roast at the same hot temperature for 15–20 minutes.

ROAST POTATOES

If you know that you are going to be very pushed on Christmas Day,
then it is possible to half-roast the potatoes the day before (see below).
On Christmas Day the potatoes simply need to be re-roasted
in a hot oven for about 20 minutes.

1.4kg (3 lb) old potatoes, such
    as Désirée, King Edward
    or Maris Piper, peeled
salt and freshly ground
    black pepper
3–4 tablespoons goose fat

Preheat the oven to 220°C/Fan 200°C/Gas 7.

STEP 1 Cut the potatoes into even-sized pieces, and put into
a large pan. Cover with cold water, add a little salt and bring
to the boil. Parboil for about 5 minutes. Drain the potatoes
well using a colander, then shake the colander to fluff up
the edges of the potatoes.

STEP 2 Heat the goose fat in a large roasting tin in the
preheated oven for about 5 minutes until piping hot. Add the
potatoes to the fat, spooning the fat over the potatoes to coat
completely, and shake the tin to prevent sticking. Continue
to roast for about an hour, depending on size, turning the
potatoes from time to time, until golden and crisp.

STEP 3 Sprinkle the roast potatoes with salt just before serving.

AGA Heat the goose fat in the
roasting tin on the floor of the
Roasting Oven until piping hot.
Add the potatoes, spooning the
fat over them to coat completely,
and shake the tin to prevent
sticking. Continue to cook on
the floor of the Roasting Oven
for about an hour, depending on
size, turning from time to time.

PREPARING AHEAD Complete
step1 then follow step 2, but
roast the potatoes for only
20–30 minutes or until they are
a pale gold. Remove any excess
fat from the tin and allow the
potatoes to cool. Keep in a cool
place overnight. On Christmas
Day, re-roast at the same hot
temperature for about 20 minutes
or until the potatoes are crisp
and golden brown. Alternatively,
you can just parboil and fluff
the potatoes ahead.

TIP Goose fat is available
at Christmas time from good
supermarkets and makes all
the difference to the flavour
of the roast potatoes. Don't
use too much, though, as
this will simply make the
potatoes go soggy.

ROASTED SWEET POTATOES AND SQUASH

V

Delicious served with a roast or on its own
with chicken breasts.

1 small butternut squash, peeled
   and cut into 2.5cm (1 in) cubes
2 large sweet potatoes, peeled
   and cut into 2.5cm (1 in) cubes
3 tablespoons olive oil
1 sprig of rosemary, leaves
   removed and finely chopped
1 tablespoon maple syrup
   or honey
salt and freshly ground
   black pepper

Preheat the oven to 220ºC/Fan 200ºC/Gas 7. Line a flat baking sheet with non-stick paper.

STEP 1 Scatter the prepared vegetables on the prepared baking sheet and drizzle over the oil and chopped rosemary leaves.

STEP 2 Roast in the oven for 25 minutes.

STEP 3 Remove from the oven and pour the maple syrup over the vegetables. Season with salt and pepper, toss and return to the oven for a further 7 minutes or until golden and caramelised.

STEP 4 Serve straight from the oven.

AGA Roast on the floor of the Roasting Oven as above.

PREPARING AHEAD Can be made up to 8 hours ahead and reheated on a flat baking sheet in a hot oven. Not suitable for freezing.

TIP Squash can be tricky to peel as it has a tough outer skin. We find it best to cut into quarters and then remove the skin with a small sharp knife.

STILTON MASH

Most of us have Stilton at Christmas, and this is a perfect way of using up any left over from the cheeseboard. Floury potatoes are the best to use, e.g. Désirée.

900g (2 lb) old potatoes
salt and freshly ground
    black pepper
about 150ml (¼ pint) hot milk
75g (3 oz) Stilton cheese,
    coarsely grated
a good handful of fresh
    parsley, chopped

STEP 1 Peel the potatoes, and cut into even-sized cubes. Cover with salted water in a saucepan, bring to the boil and boil for about 20 minutes until tender. Drain thoroughly.

STEP 2 Return the potatoes to the pan, draw to one side off the heat and add the hot milk. Return to the heat, and allow to almost boil on the hob.

STEP 3 Mash until smooth, add the Stilton, then mash again. Lighten by giving it a quick whisk with a small balloon whisk, adding a little more milk or butter if necessary. Lightly mix in the parsley and some black pepper. Serve hot.

VARIATIONS
To vary the mash, leave out the Stilton and parsley.

BACON AND ONION MASH Add 100g (4 oz) fried bacon lardons and 1 large chopped fried onion with a good knob of butter.

FRESH HERB MASH Add 2 tablespoons chopped fresh leafy herbs and a dollop of cream.

SPRING ONION MASH Finely chop 6 spring onions, including most of the green part, and add 4 tablespoons mayonnaise.

MUSTARD AND CHIVE MASH Add 2 tablespoons grainy mustard, 4 tablespoons chopped chives and a good knob of butter.

CELERIAC AND POTATO MASH Cook 450g (1 lb) each of potatoes and celeriac together in salted water, drain and mash with 200ml (7 fl oz) crème fraîche (no milk) and some black pepper.

AGA Bring the potato cubes to the boil on the Boiling Plate and cook for about 20 minutes until tender.

PREPARING AHEAD You can prepare mashes a few hours ahead of time. Cool quickly, put into a buttered shallow dish, and chill. Reheat, covered with foil, in a hot oven for about 20 minutes.

CELERIAC PURÉE

V

This is a perfect dish to be made ahead and reheated,
and is wonderful with the turkey on Christmas Day.
This purée is also excellent with roast beef.

1 × 1.8kg (4 lb) celeriac
salt and freshly ground
    black pepper
1 × 200ml (7 fl oz) carton
    full-fat crème fraîche
freshly grated nutmeg

STEP 1 Peel the thick skin off the celeriac with a knife and cut
the flesh into even-sized pieces of about 2.5cm (1 in). Boil in
salted water for 20–25 minutes until really soft. Drain well.

STEP 2 Tip the celeriac carefully into a food processor, add
the crème fraîche, salt, pepper and freshly grated nutmeg,
and blend until really smooth. Check for seasoning and
serve hot.

AGA Bring the celeriac chunks
to the boil in boiling salted
water on the Boiling Plate. Drain,
cover with a lid and transfer to
the Simmering Oven for about
50 minutes until really soft
and tender. Complete as above.
To reheat the purée, cover the
dish with foil and put into the
Simmering Oven for about 1 hour
or on the second set of runners
in the Roasting Oven for about
15 minutes.

PREPARING AHEAD The celeriac
purée can be made the day before
and reheated when needed. Allow
the purée to cool, then turn into a
buttered ovenproof dish. Cover with
clingfilm and keep in the fridge
until needed. To reheat, remove
the clingfilm, blot any excess liquid
from the sides using kitchen paper,
cover the dish with buttered foil
and put into the oven, preheated
to 190°C/Fan 170°C/Gas 5, for about
20 minutes or until piping hot.

TIP Buy celeriac at farm
shops, where you can often
find cheaper vegetables.

BRAISED RED CABBAGE

V

An ideal vegetable to prepare ahead, and it is excellent with turkey or goose.
You don't need to add any liquid to the red cabbage to cook it: if you rinse
the shredded cabbage in a colander before cooking, then a little water is
retained in the shreds.

1 large red cabbage, about 1kg
  (2¼ lb), finely shredded
450g (1 lb) cooking apples,
  peeled and roughly chopped
40g (1½ oz) caster sugar
salt and freshly ground
  black pepper
2 tablespoons white wine vinegar
50g (2 oz) butter
2 tablespoons redcurrant jelly

Preheat the oven to 150°C/Fan 130°C/Gas 2.

STEP 1 Layer the cabbage and apples in a large pan
or casserole, and add the sugar, seasoning, vinegar
and dots of butter. Gently stir to mix.

STEP 2 Cook in the preheated oven for 2–2½ hours
or until the cabbage is tender.

STEP 3 Stir in the redcurrant jelly and adjust
seasoning to taste.

AGA After step 1 bring to the
boil on the Boiling Plate, stirring
constantly for a few moments
until piping hot. Cover and
transfer to the floor of the
Simmering Oven for 2–3 hours.

PREPARING AHEAD Red cabbage
reheats beautifully. Prepare up to
2 days ahead, cool, cover and keep
in the fridge. Reheat in a large pan
for about 20 minutes until piping
hot, adding a little water or stock
if necessary. Red cabbage also
freezes well. Cool, spoon into
a freezerproof container and
freeze for up to 3 months. Thaw
overnight at cool room temperature
and reheat as above.

TIP Red cabbage also goes well
with pork and other roasts.

ROASTED ENGLISH ROOTS

V

These are perfect to go with a roast or any other meat main course. If you prefer, cut the vegetables in larger pieces, but of course they will take a little longer.

350g (12 oz) parsnips
350g (12 oz) carrots
350g (12 oz) potatoes
350g (12 oz) swede
salt and freshly ground
 black pepper
3 tablespoons olive oil
5 sprigs of fresh thyme leaves

Preheat the oven to 220ºC/Fan 200ºC/Gas 7.

STEP 1 Peel all the vegetables, and cut into 2.5cm (1 in) cubes. Blanch the prepared vegetables in boiling salted water for about 5 minutes, then drain well.

STEP 2 Measure the oil into a large roasting tin, and heat in the preheated oven for about 3 minutes until piping hot.

STEP 3 Tip the vegetables and thyme into the hot oil, season with salt and pepper, and mix until all the vegetables are coated in the oil.

STEP 4 Roast in the preheated oven for 20–30 minutes or until golden brown and cooked through.

AGA Slide the roasting tin directly on to the floor of the Roasting Oven for about 15 minutes, turning over halfway through.

PREPARING AHEAD You can roast the vegetables well in advance, but slightly undercook them. Leave them in the roasting tin, and return to the oven for about 20 minutes before serving.

TIP You can use a variety of root vegetables in this way. Swede, turnips, pumpkin and sweet potatoes will all roast very well. The essential thing is to use a large roasting tin and space the vegetables out well. If they are piled on top of each other they will just go soggy and not become crisp.

BEETROOT AND HORSERADISH

V

A delicious dish to serve alongside roast beef. Buy cooked fresh beetroot with the skin on, not the pickled beetroot from a jar as these will break up on cooking.

6 medium cooked beetroot
½ × 185g (6½ oz) jar creamed
  horseradish

Preheat the oven to 180ºC/Fan 160ºC/Gas 4.

STEP 1 Peel the beetroot (wearing gloves) and cut into short strips the thickness of a pencil. Mix in a bowl with the horseradish, season and then transfer to an ovenproof dish.

STEP 2 Cover the dish with foil and roast in the oven for 20 minutes until piping hot, stirring occasionally.

AGA Cook in the Roasting Oven for 20 minutes.

PREPARING AHEAD Make the beetroot and horseradish earlier in the day or the day before

TIP Creamed horseradish is much milder than horseradish in a jar so be careful to buy the right one.

PARISIENNE POTATOES

V

So often when potatoes, onion and cream are cooked together, you end up with the cream curdling. But in this recipe, because the potatoes and onions are boiled ahead, you will not have that problem. I'm afraid this is not a recipe for dieters, but you can always opt for a very small portion...

1.5 kg (3¼ lb) potatoes
1 large onion, sliced into
 about 14 wedges
salt and freshly ground
 black pepper
300ml (½ pint) double cream
75g (3 oz) Gruyère cheese, grated

Preheat the oven to 200ºC/Fan 180ºC/Gas 6.

STEP 1 Peel the potatoes and cut into 2.5cm (1 in) cubes or thick slices.

STEP 2 Put the potatoes and onion into a pan, cover with cold salted water and boil for about 10 minutes or until the potatoes are just cooked.

STEP 3 Drain and pour into a shallow buttered ovenproof dish, season with salt and pepper and pour over the cream.

STEP 4 Sprinkle with the cheese and cook in the preheated oven for 15–20 minutes or until golden brown and bubbling.

AGA Cook in the Roasting Oven towards the top for about 15 minutes.

PREPARING AHEAD You can do quite a lot of the dish up to 12 hours in advance. Boil the potatoes and onion, turn into the dish and season. Just before going into the oven, pour over the cream, and top with cheese. If cooking from cold, the cooking time will be about 10 minutes longer.

TIP Use main-crop potatoes, such as King Edward or Maris Piper, because they don't break up in cooking. Don't attempt to use single cream here because the consistency will be wrong.

SAVOY, SPINACH AND LEEK STIR-FRY WITH A HINT OF ORANGE

V

A quick stir-fry as an alternative vegetable. The orange gives it an out-of-the-ordinary flavour.

450g (1 lb) Savoy cabbage
225g (8 oz) baby spinach
1 large leek
25g (1 oz) butter
finely grated zest and juice
    of 1 small orange
salt and freshly ground
    black pepper

STEP 1 First prepare the vegetables. Cut the cabbage into quarters, remove the core and very finely slice. Remove any coarse stalks from the spinach, and wash the leaves. Shred finely. Cut the leek in half lengthways, then in half again, and slice into very thin batons. Wash and drain thoroughly.

STEP 2 Melt the butter in a large deep frying pan over a high heat. Stir in the cabbage and leek and stir-fry for 3–4 minutes. Add the baby spinach, orange zest and juice, and season with plenty of salt and pepper. Fry for a further 2 minutes until the spinach has wilted.

STEP 3 Pile the vegetables into a warm serving dish and serve at once.

AGA Stir-fry on the Boiling Plate as above.

PREPARING AHEAD All the vegetables can be prepared up to 8 hours before, and kept separately in the fridge.

TIP I adore pointed cabbages, and they work very well with this recipe too.

TRADITIONAL CHRISTMAS PUDDINGS

CHAPTER SIX

I know calories and overindulgence are a concern to us all, particularly during the festive season, but I still think puddings and desserts are an essential part of Christmas eating and pleasure. A Christmas lunch just wouldn't be the same for me if it didn't finish with a traditional steamed pudding, served with a boozy sauce. I've given you a new recipe here, which can be made at least 6–8 weeks in advance, but there are also plenty of other Christmas favourites. You can serve a hot pudding – much appreciated in the cold winter months – and a cold one – after all, Christmas comes but once a year! I always say that Christmas just isn't Christmas without a traditional trifle, and I've included my favourite trifle recipe here.

CHRISTMAS PUDDING

Traditionally, Christmas pudding is made on 'Stir-up Sunday' at the end of November. However, the pudding can be made earlier than this if more convenient: feed it with a little more brandy or rum once it is cooked and cold, and keep in a cool place until Christmas Day.

75g (3 oz) butter, softened, plus extra for greasing
450g (1 lb) dried fruit (use a mixture of sultanas, raisins and snipped apricots)
1 small cooking apple, peeled, cored and roughly chopped (about 175g/6 oz)
finely grated rind and juice of 1 orange
50ml (2 fl oz) brandy or rum, plus extra for feeding and flaming
100g (4 oz) light muscovado sugar
2 eggs
100g (4 oz) self-raising flour
1 level teaspoon ground mixed spice
40g (1½ oz) fresh white breadcrumbs
40g (1½ oz) whole shelled almonds, roughly chopped

Lightly butter a 1.4 litre (2½ pint) pudding basin. Cut a small square of foil and press into the base of the basin.

STEP 1 Measure the sultanas, raisins, apricots and apple into a bowl with the orange juice. Add the measured brandy or rum and leave to marinate for about 1 hour.

STEP 2 Put the measured butter, sugar and grated orange rind into a large bowl and cream together with a wooden spoon or a hand-held electric whisk until light and fluffy. Gradually beat in the eggs, adding a little flour if the mixture starts to curdle.

STEP 3 Sift together the flour and mixed spice, then fold into the creamed mixture with the breadcrumbs and the nuts. Add the dried fruits, apple and liquid and stir well.

STEP 4 Spoon into the prepared pudding basin, pressing the mixture down, and level the top with the back of a spoon. Cover the pudding with a layer of greaseproof paper and foil, both pleated across the middle to allow for expansion. Tie securely with string and trim off excess paper and foil with scissors.

Recipe continued overleaf

Recipe continued

STEP 5 To steam, put the pudding in the top of a steamer filled with simmering water, cover with a lid and steam for about 8 hours, topping up the water as necessary. To boil the pudding, put a metal jam-jar lid into the base of a large pan to act as a trivet. Put the pudding on to this and pour in enough boiling water to come one-third of the way up the bowl. Cover with a lid, bring the water back to the boil, then simmer for about 7 hours, until the pudding is a glorious deep brown colour, topping up the water as necessary.

STEP 6 Remove the pudding from the steamer or pan and cool completely. Make holes in the pudding with a fine skewer and pour in a little more brandy or rum to feed. Discard the paper and foil and replace with fresh. Store in a cool, dry place.

STEP 7 On Christmas Day, steam or boil the pudding for about an hour to reheat. Turn the pudding on to a serving plate. To flame, warm 3–4 tablespoons brandy or rum in a small pan, pour it over the hot pudding and set light to it. Serve with Rum Sauce, Boozy Cream or Brandy Butter (see pages 150–1).

AGA To cook, bring to the boil on the Boiling Plate, cover with a lid and transfer to the Simmering Oven for about 12 hours. To reheat, tightly wrap the cooked pudding, in its bowl, in a double layer of foil and sit it next to the turkey in the Simmering Oven, from early morning. Leave it for several hours and it will slowly reheat and be piping hot at the end of the meal.

PREPARING AHEAD Make and cook the pudding 6–8 weeks before Christmas. As it does take a fair time to steam, make things easier for yourself by preparing the pudding up to the end of step 4 the day before. Keep the pudding in a cool place overnight, and steam as directed the next day. Cover the cold pudding with fresh greaseproof paper and foil and store in a cool place until Christmas. You can also freeze Christmas pudding, but as it stores so well it doesn't seem worth it! If it really helps you to freeze it, then allow it to mature for a month before freezing.

TIP It is quite useful to use a see-through bowl for the pudding as you can then check the colour as it is cooking. Any leftover Christmas pudding can be wrapped in foil and reheated in a medium oven for about 30 minutes.

RUM SAUCE

This is quite old fashioned but often popular with the older generation.

75g (3 oz) butter
40g (1½ oz) plain flour
900ml (1½ pints) milk
50g (2 oz) caster sugar
4–6 tablespoons rum

STEP 1 Melt the butter in a small pan then stir in the flour. Gradually add the milk, stirring constantly. Bring to the boil.

STEP 2 Stir in the sugar and simmer very gently for about 2 minutes, stirring occasionally.

STEP 3 Add the rum to taste, pour into a warmed serving jug and serve hot with the Christmas pudding.

AGA Make on the Simmering Plate.

PREPARING AHEAD This is best served freshly made.

TIP If you prefer brandy sauce, add brandy instead of rum.

BOOZY CREAM

This is wonderful with Christmas pudding, mince pies or chocolate roulade, and is delicious with fruit salad too! Indulge in your favourite tipple – Bailey's, rum, brandy, Grand Marnier or Cointreau.

300ml (½ pint) double cream
25g (1 oz) caster sugar or icing sugar
1–3 tablespoons liqueur of choice (see above)

STEP 1 Whip the cream with the sugar to form soft peaks.

STEP 2 Fold in your chosen booze to taste: 1 tablespoon is good, 2 tablespoons even better, and 3 tablespoons – wow!

PREPARING AHEAD Prepare up to 4 hours ahead, and keep covered in the fridge.

TIP If you are using an orange-based liqueur such as Grand Marnier or Cointreau, then add the finely grated rind of an orange to the cream for extra flavour.

BRANDY BUTTER

Brandy butter is delicious with mince pies, Christmas pudding, Christmas Tarte Amandine (see page 158), Apple, Lemon and Cinnamon Strudel (see page 173) or even spread on to crumpets.

100g (4 oz) unsalted butter, softened
225g (8 oz) icing sugar, sieved
3–5 tablespoons brandy or Cognac

STEP 1 Measure the butter into a bowl. Beat well with a wooden spoon until soft – or for speed use an electric hand whisk (or processor, see Tip). Beat in the sieved icing sugar until smooth, then add brandy or Cognac to taste.

STEP 2 Spoon into a serving dish, cover and keep in the fridge.

PREPARING AHEAD Brandy butter keeps well, up to 2 weeks in the fridge. It also freezes. Spoon into a freezerproof container and freeze for up to 1 month. Thaw overnight at cool room temperature.

TIP If you are making brandy butter in the processor, you don't need to sieve the icing sugar. Just mix the butter and sugar, then add the brandy at the end. Another very worthwhile tip is that if you use hard butter, then you can use more brandy, although you must use a processor. But if you are over-generous with the brandy, the mixture will curdle: simply beat in more sieved icing sugar, and it will come smooth again.

MINCE PIES

These are traditional mince pies with a pastry top and bottom, but I have used a star cutter for the top – so much more festive and slightly less pastry too! If you are feeling very creative, you could also cut out holly or Christmas tree shapes and use these to top the mince pies.

about 350g (12 oz) mincemeat
1 egg, beaten, to glaze
icing or caster sugar for dusting

PASTRY
175g (6 oz) plain flour
75g (3 oz) butter, cut into cubes
25g (1 oz) icing sugar
finely grated rind of 1 orange
1 egg, beaten

STEP 1 To make the pastry, measure the flour, butter, icing sugar and grated orange rind into a food processor bowl and process until the mixture resembles breadcrumbs. Pour in the beaten egg and pulse the blade until the dough starts to form a ball. Knead lightly by hand on a floured board.

Preheat the oven to 200°C/Fan 180°C/Gas 6.

STEP 2 Roll the pastry out thinly on a lightly floured work surface and cut out 18 rounds using a 7.5cm (3 in) fluted cutter. Use these to line 18 holes of two 12-hole bun tins. Spoon a generously heaped teaspoon of mincemeat into each pastry case.

STEP 3 Re-roll the pastry trimmings and cut out 18 stars using a 4.5 –5cm (1¾–2 in) star cutter. Put a star on top of the mincemeat, and brush the pastry with a little beaten egg.

STEP 4 Bake in the preheated oven for 12–15 minutes or until golden and crisp. Allow to cool slightly and dust with icing sugar or caster sugar before serving.

AGA Bake the mince pies on the grid shelf on the floor of the Roasting Oven for 10–15 minutes using the cold plain shelf if they are becoming too brown. Turn the pies around halfway through.

PREPARING AHEAD Bake the mince pies but don't dust with icing sugar. Store in an airtight container for up to 3 days. When needed, place on a baking tray and reheat in the oven preheated to 160°C/Fan 140°C/Gas 3 for 8–10 minutes. To freeze the pies after baking, prepare to the end of step 4 but don't dust with sugar. Pack into a rigid plastic container and freeze for up to a month. Thaw at room temperature for 2–3 hours, then warm through as directed above.

TIP These are best served warm, and are delicious with Brandy Butter or Boozy Cream (see pages 151 and 150).

SPECIAL MINCEMEAT

I prefer the flavour of butter to suet in mincemeat – which makes it suitable for vegetarians – but use suet if you wish. The butter makes the mincemeat look slightly cloudy in the jar but this disappears once the mincemeat is cooked in mince pies, etc.

175g (6 oz) currants
175g (6 oz) raisins
175g (6 oz) sultanas
175g (6 oz) dried cranberries
100g (4 oz) mixed peel
1 small cooking apple, peeled, cored and finely chopped
125g (4 oz) butter, cut into cubes
50g (2 oz) whole blanched almonds, roughly chopped
225g (8 oz) light muscovado sugar
½ teaspoon ground cinnamon
1 teaspoon mixed spice
finely grated rind and juice of 1 lemon
200ml (7 fl oz) brandy, rum or sherry

STEP 1 Measure all of the ingredients except the alcohol into a large pan. Heat gently, allowing the butter to melt, then simmer very gently, stirring occasionally, for about 10 minutes.

STEP 2 Allow the mixture to cool completely then stir in the brandy, rum or sherry.

STEP 3 Spoon the mincemeat into sterilised jam jars, seal tightly, label and store in a cool place.

AGA Follow step 1, heat gently on the Boiling Plate, cover and transfer to the Simmering Oven for about 20 minutes.

PREPARING AHEAD Make the mincemeat up to 6 months ahead, and store in a cool place. It's not necessary to freeze mincemeat as it stores so well.

TIP I no longer use cellophane tops or wax paper. I simply use clean, sterilised screw-top jars saved from bought marmalade or jam.

FRANGIPANE MINCE PIES

A new variation on an old favourite. You will need deep mince pie tins for 18 pies and a 6.5cm (2½ in) cutter.

PASTRY
175g (6 oz) plain flour
75g (3 oz) butter, cut into cubes
25g (1 oz) icing sugar
1 egg, beaten

FRANGIPANE
100g (4 oz) butter, softened
100g (4 oz) caster sugar
2 large eggs
100g (4 oz) ground almonds
1 level tablespoon plain flour
½ teaspoon almond extract,
    or to taste

FILLING AND TOPPING
just under 1 × 410g (14 oz) jar
    mincemeat flavoured with
    about 2 tablespoons brandy
a few flaked almonds
apricot jam to glaze
lemon juice

VARIATION
If you want to make a large tart you can use the exact quantity above to fill a 23cm (9 in) loose-bottomed flan tin, which will take about 25 minutes in the preheated oven.

Preheat the oven to 200ºC/Fan 180ºC/Gas 6.

STEP 1 To make the pastry, measure the flour, butter and icing sugar into a food processor bowl, then process until the mixture resembles breadcrumbs. Pour in the beaten egg and pulse the blade until the dough starts to form a ball. Knead lightly, wrap and chill for about 30 minutes if the pastry is not quite firm enough to roll out.

STEP 2 To make the frangipane, measure the butter and sugar into the unwashed processor, and blend until soft and creamy. Scrape down the sides, add the eggs and continue to process. Don't worry if the mixture looks curdled at this stage. Add the ground almonds, flour and almond extract, and mix briefly.

STEP 3 Roll the pastry out thinly on a lightly floured work surface and cut into eighteen 6.5cm (2½ in) circles. Use to line the tins. Spoon a teaspoon of mincemeat into each tartlet and top with the frangipane mixture. There is no need to spread the mixture flat as it will level out in the oven (but do not overfill the tins). Sprinkle a few flaked almonds on top.

STEP 4 Bake in the preheated oven for 15–17 minutes, watching carefully. Remove from the tins and allow to cool a little on a wire rack.

STEP 5 Dilute the apricot jam with a little lemon juice or water and bring to the boil. Brush each warm tartlet with glaze. Like traditional mince pies, these are best served warm.

AGA Bake on the floor of the Roasting Oven for about 8 minutes to brown the pastry base. Turn round and slide on the grid shelf on the floor of the Roasting Oven for a further 6–8 minutes until well risen and golden brown. Put the cold plain shelf on the second set of runners if getting too brown.

PREPARING AHEAD Complete to the end of step 4 up to 3 days ahead. Refresh in a moderate oven at 180ºC/Fan 160ºC/Gas 4 for 8–10 minutes, then glaze. Freeze the mince pies at the end of step 4. Thaw at room temperature for 2–3 hours. Warm through in the oven as above, then glaze.

CHRISTMAS TARTE AMANDINE

This tart is very special, and will feed many guests over Christmas. It freezes well too. Use a bought 500g (1 lb 2 oz) pack of shortcrust pastry if time is short.

PASTRY
225g (8 oz) plain flour
100g (4 oz) butter, cubed
50g (2 oz) caster sugar
1 egg
1 tablespoon water

ALMOND FILLING
175g (6 oz) butter
175g (6 oz) caster sugar
4 eggs
175g (6 oz) ground almonds
1 teaspoon almond extract
a generous ½ jar good-quality
    mincemeat

TOPPING
about 75g (3 oz) icing sugar
juice of ½ lemon
about 50g (2 oz) flaked almonds

Preheat the oven to 190ºC/Fan 170ºC/Gas 5, and put a heavy, flat baking tray into it to heat up.

STEP 1 First make the pastry, either by the usual rubbing-in method by hand or measure the flour and butter into a processor and process until rubbed in. Add the sugar and mix for a moment, then add the egg and water. Process until the mixture just holds together.

STEP 2 Roll the pastry out on a floured surface and use to line a 28cm (11 in) flan tin. There will be ample pastry. Prick the base of the pastry using a fork.

STEP 3 Next make the filling – no need to wash up the processor. Process the butter and sugar until creamy, add the eggs and blend, then mix in the ground almonds and almond extract.

STEP 4 Spread a thin layer of mincemeat over the base of the pastry and spoon the almond mixture on top.

STEP 5 Sit the tart tin on the hot baking sheet, and bake in the preheated oven for 45–50 minutes until the pastry is crisp and golden brown.

STEP 6 To finish the tart, make a glacé icing from the icing sugar and lemon juice, adding water to make it a pouring consistency. Spread over the tart and sprinkle with flaked almonds. Return to the oven for about 5 minutes.

AGA Bake on the floor of the Roasting Oven for about 25 minutes or until golden and firm in the centre. After about 10 minutes, slide the cold plain shelf above on the second set of runners to prevent the tart getting too brown. When the tart is iced, put it on a baking sheet and slide on to the grid shelf on the second set of runners in the Roasting Oven for about 5 minutes to give a shiny top and to lightly colour the almonds.

PREPARING AHEAD The pastry-lined flan tin can be kept, covered with clingfilm, in the fridge for up to 12 hours. Filled with the mincemeat and almond filling, it can be kept for about 1 hour, covered and refrigerated. You can also freeze the tart, after the end of step 6. Cool, wrap and freeze for up to 1 month.

ICE CREAM CHRISTMAS PUDDING

A wonderful alternative Christmas pudding. It contains raw eggs so is not suitable for pregnant ladies or the very young or elderly. If you can see flecks of butter or fat in the mincemeat, heat until the fat has melted, then cool before adding to the cream.

1 × 450g (1 lb) jar vegetarian suet-free mincemeat
3 tablespoons rum
4 eggs
300ml (½ pint) double cream
100g (4 oz) caster sugar

VARIATION
If you prefer, you can use brandy instead of rum.

STEP 1 Line a 2 litre (3½ pint) pudding basin with cling film.

STEP 2 Mix the mincemeat and rum together.

STEP 3 Separate the eggs. Place the yolks in a small bowl and mix until well blended. Whisk the cream until it forms soft peaks. Using an electric mixer, whisk the egg whites on fast speed until stiff, then gradually add the sugar a teaspoonful at a time, still on fast speed. You may need to scrape down the sides of the bowl from time to time.

STEP 4 Fold the egg yolks and cream into the meringue, followed by the brandy and mincemeat.

STEP 5 Turn the ice cream mixture into the pudding basin, cover and freeze overnight.

STEP 6 To turn the pudding out, dip the basin in very hot water for a few moments and turn upside down on to a serving plate – just as you would with a jelly. Remove the cling film and serve with Toffee Sauce or Rum and Raisin Sauce (see page 172).

PREPARING AHEAD
The ice cream can be frozen for up to 1 month.

CLASSIC OLD-FASHIONED TRIFLE

It wouldn't be Christmas without trifle! This is a good traditional recipe which is always popular with my family. There are now some very good-quality ready-made fresh vanilla custards available in the chilled cabinet at good supermarkets, but of course you can make your own fresh custard if you prefer.

1 × 400g (14 oz) can pears
in natural juice
1 packet trifle sponges,
containing 8 sponges
strawberry jam
75ml (3 fl oz) medium dry sherry
about 10 ratafia biscuits,
or broken almond biscuits
such as macaroons
600ml (1 pint) bought good-
quality fresh vanilla custard
300ml (½ pint) double cream
25g (1 oz) flaked almonds,
lightly toasted (and see Tip)

STEP 1 Drain the pears, reserving the juice, then cut the fruit into small pieces. Split the trifle sponges in half and sandwich together with strawberry jam. Measure the sherry into a jug and make up to 150ml (¼ pint) with the reserved pear juice. If you don't wish to have sherry in your trifle, then use all of the pear juice – about 150ml (¼ pint).

STEP 2 Put half of the chopped pears into the base of a shallow glass serving dish about 20cm (8 in) in diameter and 6cm (2½ in) deep. Arrange half of the trifle sponges on top, then add the remaining pears and finally the remaining trifle sponges. Scatter the ratafias on top and pour the sherry and pear juice mixture over evenly.

STEP 3 Carefully pour the custard over the top. Lightly whip the cream until it just holds its shape and spoon over the custard. Gently level the surface. Sprinkle with the toasted flaked almonds just before serving. Serve chilled.

PREPARING AHEAD This is an ideal dessert to make a day ahead as the flavours have time to mingle. Keep in the fridge. Scatter over the toasted flaked almonds just before serving.

TIP Flaked almonds can now be bought ready toasted but, if you do need to toast them yourself, put them in a dry pan over a medium heat on the hob. Move them around with a wooden spoon and watch them like a hawk as they can quickly burn.

VODKA TRIFLE WITH CHERRIES AND ORANGE

This trifle is very colourful as well as delicious. It is best made the day before, so that the flavours have time to develop. Trifle sponges come in packets of eight: you'll find them in the supermarket, usually in the custards and jelly section.

1 × 250g (9 oz) tub mascarpone cheese, at room temperature
4 tablespoons vodka
finely grated zest of 2 oranges
300ml (½ pint) double cream, lightly whisked
12 – 16 trifle sponges
⅔ × 600g (1 1b 5 oz) jar Bonne Maman cherry compote
3 oranges, peeled and segmented
8 Cape gooseberries to decorate
icing sugar

STEP 1 Measure the mascarpone, vodka and half the orange zest into a mixing bowl. Add the cream a little at a time to the cheese, beating well until smooth.

STEP 2 Split the trifle sponges horizontally.

STEP 3 Spread half of the cheese mixture across the bottom of a round 26cm (10½ in) shallow glass dish. Arrange half of the split sponges on the cheese mixture and press down gently. (The number of sponges you use will vary with the size of the dish you have.) Spoon the cherry compote on top, spreading right to the edges of the bowl. Arrange the orange segments on top and the remaining trifle sponges on the fruit. Spread the remaining cheese mixture over the surface.

STEP 4 Scatter the reserved orange zest over the trifle, cover with clingfilm and leave in the fridge for the sponges to soak, ideally overnight.

STEP 5 The next day, arrange the Cape gooseberries around the edge. Dust with a little icing sugar just before serving.

PREPARING AHEAD This must be made a day in advance.

TIP Cape gooseberries are also called physalis and Chinese lanterns. They are small golden berries with a thin papery husk which for decoration is folded back to expose the berry, and looks most attractive and delicious to eat.

FESTIVE DESSERTS

CHAPTER SEVEN

Plum pudding isn't for everyone, I know, so I wanted
to include some festive and celebratory desserts for
those of you who usually avoid the traditional dishes
on Christmas Day. They would also be good if you are
looking for something a bit different for a New Year
gathering. Orange Panna Cotta would be an unexpected
but lovely addition to a cold buffet selection, while the
Divine White Chocolate Cheesecake is a real crowd
pleaser and, because it is so rich, a little goes a long way.
You'll also find some ideas here about what to do with
your mincemeat other than make mince pies; try the
Mincemeat Bread and Butter Pudding or the Mincemeat
and Apple Caramel. People think making dessert is going
to take too much time, especially at Christmas, when
there is so much else to do. But many of the recipes
here – not just the ice cream – can be made well ahead,
and frozen, like the Apple, Lemon and Cinnamon
Strudel. When it's a time to celebrate, you can
afford a bit of indulgence!

GINGER SPICED PUDDING

Delicious served cold as a cake without a toffee sauce, or warm as a pudding, as below. I prefer it warm with the sauce, and like to serve slices of fresh mango with it too.

50g (2 oz) butter, melted,
   plus extra for greasing
100g (4 oz) light muscovado
   sugar, plus extra for dusting
100g (4 oz) plain flour
½ teaspoon bicarbonate of soda
2 teaspoons ground cinnamon
1 teaspoon ground ginger
¼ teaspoon freshly grated nutmeg
1 egg, beaten
75g (3 oz) black treacle
125ml (4½ fl oz) milk

TO SERVE
1 mango, cut into thin slices
1 recipe toffee sauce
   (see page 172)

Preheat the oven to 180°C/Fan 160°C/Gas 4. You will need a 1kg (2 lb) loaf tin, which you should generously butter and dust with light muscovado sugar.

STEP 1 Measure all the dry ingredients, except for the sugar, into a large bowl. In a separate bowl mix the egg, sugar, treacle, milk and melted butter together and beat until smooth and there are no lumps.

STEP 2 Stir the wet ingredients into the dry ingredients and beat hard for about a minute until smooth. Pour into the loaf tin (it will only part-fill the tin).

STEP 3 Bake in the preheated oven for about 35 minutes until dark in colour, shrinking away from the sides of the tin and springy to the touch. Cover loosely with foil if getting too dark.

STEP 4 Arrange slices of mango on a plate and sit a slice of ginger pudding on top. Serve warm with warm toffee sauce.

AGA Put the small grill rack upside down in a small roasting tin. Sit the loaf tin on top and slide on to the grid shelf on the floor of the Roasting Oven with the cold plain shelf on the second set of runners for about 25–30 minutes.

TIP We also tested this recipe using self-raising flour and no bicarbonate of soda. It worked well but we preferred the sticky texture with bicarbonate of soda. The loaf will be very shallow – when we cooked it in a 450g (1 lb) loaf tin, it overflowed.

TOFFEE SAUCE

The children especially enjoy this sauce, and it disappears
from the jar so quickly that I keep it hidden at the
back of the fridge!

50g (2 oz) butter
75g (3 oz) caster sugar
50g (2 oz) light muscovado sugar
150g (5 oz) golden syrup
1 x 170g (7 oz) can evaporated milk

STEP 1 Put the butter, sugars and syrup in a pan and heat
gently until melted and liquid, stirring continuously.
Boil gently for 5 minutes.

STEP 2 Remove the pan from the heat and gradually stir
in the evaporated milk. The sauce is now ready and can
be served hot or warm, or dolloped on cold.

AGA Start off on the
Simmering Plate, then
transfer to the Boiling Plate
and boil gently for 5 minutes.

PREPARING AHEAD Keep
in the fridge for 1 month.

RUM AND RAISIN SAUCE

This is divine on any good vanilla or coffee ice cream.

225g (8 oz) granulated sugar
6 tablespoons water
225g (8 oz) raisins
75ml (2½ fl oz) rum

STEP 1 Measure the sugar and water into a medium-sized
pan, and stir over a low heat until the sugar is completely
dissolved.

STEP 2 When the syrup is completely clear, stir in the raisins
and continue to heat until they are hot. Remove the pan
from the heat and add the rum. Set aside to cool.

STEP 3 Pour into two clean jars. Leave for at least 24 hours.

AGA Make on the
Simmering Plate.

PREPARING AHEAD If the
sauce crystallises in the jar,
just reheat it in a pan until
the crystals are dissolved.

TIP Make with brandy
instead of rum.

APPLE, LEMON AND CINNAMON STRUDEL

An apple strudel used to be such a popular recipe, and we think it's worth a comeback. It is so quick and easy to make too. The breadcrumbs help to absorb some of the liquid from the apples, and stop the pastry going soggy.

about 6 sheets filo pastry (if the pastry is very thin, use 9 sheets)
about 50g (2 oz) butter, melted
about 25g (1 oz) fresh breadcrumbs

FILLING

1 large cooking apple (about 400g/14 oz peeled weight), peeled, cored and sliced
finely grated zest and juice of ½ lemon
50g (2 oz) Demerara sugar
1 teaspoon mixed spice
1 teaspoon ground cinnamon
50g (2 oz) sultanas

ICING

a little lemon juice
175g (6 oz) icing sugar, sieved

Lightly grease a baking tray. Preheat the oven to 190°C/Fan 170°C/Gas 5.

STEP 1 Mix all the filling ingredients together in a bowl.

STEP 2 Place 3 sheets of filo, long sides together, side by side on a board, slightly overlapping in the middle where they join. They should measure about 45 × 31cm (18 × 12 in) altogether. Brush with melted butter. Repeat with another one or two layers, buttering in between the pastry, using the total of 6 or 9 sheets. Sprinkle the top sheets with the breadcrumbs.

STEP 3 Spoon the filling into a third of the rectangle at the bottom of one end of the pastry (across the join) about 5cm (2 in) away from the edge and side. Cut away about 2.5cm (1 in) of pastry at the sides, from the top of the filling upwards (this helps prevent too much pastry being folded together).

STEP 4 Turn the sides in over the filling and roll up from the filling end into a sausage shape. Carefully lift the strudel on to the baking tray and brush all over with melted butter.

STEP 5 Bake in the preheated oven for about 35–40 minutes until the pastry is golden and crisp.

STEP 6 Mix the lemon juice with the sieved icing sugar (do not make it too runny or it will slide off the strudel). Drizzle in a zigzag pattern over the top of the strudel. Serve immediately with good vanilla ice cream or crème fraîche.

AGA Cook on the floor of the Roasting Oven for about 8 minutes or until the bottom of the pastry is brown. Transfer to the grid shelf on the floor of the Roasting Oven for a further 10–12 minutes until golden brown. If getting too brown, slide the cold plain shelf on to the second set of runners.

PREPARING AHEAD Prepare the strudel to the end of step 4. Cover and leave in a cool place for up to 8 hours before baking as in step 5, and icing. The strudel freezes well after cooking too. Cool the un-iced strudel, then wrap and freeze for up to 3 months. Defrost at room temperature and reheat covered in foil in a moderate oven at 180°C/Fan 160°C/Gas 4 for 10–15 minutes. Then ice.

MINCEMEAT BREAD AND BUTTER PUDDING

This is wonderful at any time of the year, not just at Christmas! It is essential to make it in a shallow dish so that you get maximum crunchy top. It rises like a soufflé, so serve at once straight from the oven.

50g (2 oz) ready-to-eat dried apricots
2 tablespoons brandy or rum
12 thin slices white bread, buttered
1 × 450g (1 lb) jar luxury mincemeat
50g (2 oz) caster sugar
3 large eggs
300ml (½ pint) double cream
1 teaspoon vanilla extract
150ml (¼ pint) milk
1 tablespoon Demerara sugar

Well butter a 28cm (11 in) fairly shallow round china ovenproof dish. Preheat the oven to 180°C/Fan 160°C/Gas 4.

STEP 1 Snip the apricots into smallish pieces and soak in the brandy or rum while making the pudding.

STEP 2 Make sandwiches of the bread using the mincemeat, but don't fill right to the edges because these are trimmed off. Cut off the crusts and cut each sandwich diagonally into four. Arrange the sandwich triangles across the dish, slightly overlapping.

STEP 3 Beat together the caster sugar, eggs, cream and vanilla extract. Stir in the milk.

STEP 4 Scatter the apricots over the bread. Gradually pour over the cream mixture, making sure all the bread is coated. If you have time, leave the pudding to stand for 30–60 minutes (to allow the bread to absorb the liquid, so it becomes light and crisp during cooking). If you have no time, don't worry – you can still bake it straightaway.

STEP 5 Sprinkle the Demerara sugar over the top of the pudding, and bake in the preheated oven for about 40 minutes until well risen, crisp and golden. Serve warm with crème fraîche or cream.

AGA Bake on the grid shelf on the floor of the Roasting Oven, with the cold plain shelf on the second set of runners, for about 25 minutes.

PREPARING AHEAD Complete to the end of step 4 up to 12 hours ahead, cover with clingfilm and leave in the fridge. Continue with step 5.

MINCEMEAT AND APPLE CARAMEL

Use dessert or cooking apples, whichever you have to hand. This is the sort of recipe that you can assemble in 10 minutes and cook for Sunday pud! You can use suet-free vegetarian mincemeat if you like.

175g (6 oz) self-raising flour
1 teaspoon baking powder
50g (2 oz) caster sugar
50g (2 oz) soft baking margarine
1 egg
finely grated rind of 1 lemon
100ml (3½ fl oz) milk
225g (8 oz) mincemeat
450g (1 lb) apples (peeled weight),
    sliced (toss in a little lemon
    juice if preparing ahead)

TOPPING
50g (2 oz) butter, melted
about 175g (6 oz) Demerara sugar

Preheat the oven to 200°C/Fan 180°C/Gas 6. Well grease a shallow round 28cm (11 in) ovenproof dish.

STEP 1 Measure the flour, baking powder, caster sugar, margarine, egg and lemon rind into a bowl. Beat well together, add the milk, and beat again until the consistency of a sponge mixture.

STEP 2 Spread the mixture on the base of the dish, spread over the mincemeat and arrange the apples on top. Brush or drizzle butter over the apples and sprinkle with Demerara sugar.

STEP 3 Bake in the preheated oven for about 35 minutes until the apples are cooked and the sponge is golden brown.

STEP 4 Serve warm with crème fraîche or cream.

AGA Slide on to the grid shelf on the floor of the Roasting Oven and bake for about 25 minutes until the apples are cooked and the sponge is golden brown. If getting too brown, slide the cold plain shelf on to the second set of runners.

PREPARING AHEAD Make the sponge mixture and spread it in the dish. Cover with clingfilm and keep in the fridge for up to 8 hours. Prepare the apples and finish the topping just before baking.

THE VERY BEST APPLE DESSERT CAKE

I've been doing this special and remarkably easy recipe for years. The apples can be windfalls or even shrivelled ones left in the fruit bowl. Serve warm with ice cream or crème fraîche as a dessert, or with coffee in the morning as one would a Danish pastry, again warm, dusted with icing sugar.

225g (8 oz) self-raising flour
1 level teaspoon baking powder
225g (8 oz) caster sugar
2 eggs
½ teaspoon almond extract
150g (5 oz) butter, melted
350g (12 oz) cooking apples,
   peeled and cored
25g (1 oz) flaked almonds

Preheat the oven to 160°C/Fan 140°C/Gas 3. Lightly grease a deep 20cm (8in) loose-bottomed cake tin.

STEP 1 Measure the flour, baking powder, sugar, eggs, almond extract and melted butter into a bowl. Mix well until blended, then beat for a minute.

STEP 2 Spread half this mixture into the prepared tin. Thickly slice the apples and lay on top of the mixture in the tin, piling mostly towards the centre. Using 2 dessertspoons, roughly spoon the remaining mixture over the apples. This is an awkward thing to do, but just make sure that the mixture covers the centre well as it will spread out in the oven. Sprinkle with the flaked almonds.

STEP 3 Bake in the preheated oven for 1¼–1½ hours until golden and coming away from the sides of the tin.

AGA With the grid shelf on the floor of the Roasting Oven and the cold plain shelf on the second set of runners, cook the cake for about 20 minutes or until pale golden brown, watching carefully. Transfer the plain shelf (which is very hot!) to the middle of the Simmering Oven, then lift the cake very carefully on to this and bake for a further 30–40 minutes or until a skewer comes out clean when inserted into the centre of the cake.

PREPARING AHEAD Best made to serve warm but can be made the day before. And, once cooked and cold, you can wrap and freeze it for a maximum of 3 months.

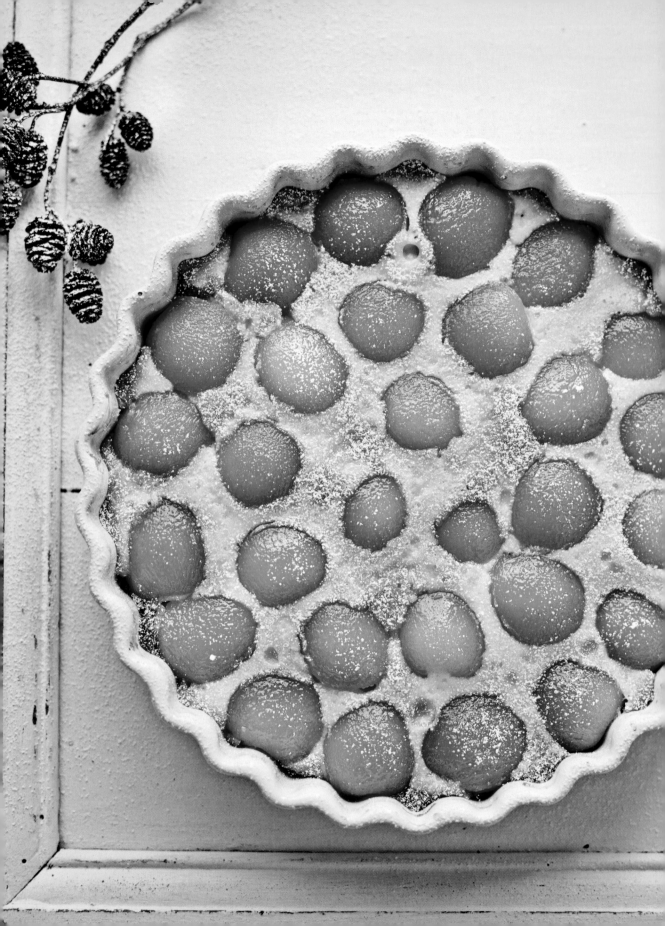

APRICOT BRIOCHE TART

A wonderfully quick and easy tart, which is good made with canned pears as well. If I were giving a numerical rating to this recipe, I would give it ten out of ten!

butter for greasing
1 egg
2 tablespoons caster sugar
1 × 250g (9 oz) tub full fat mascarpone cheese
about 225g (8 oz) brioche, sliced about 1cm (½ in) thick from a loaf
2 × 400g (14 oz) cans apricot halves, drained
about 4 tablespoons Demerara sugar
icing sugar for dusting

Well butter an ovenproof, shallow-sided dish, about 28cm (11 in) in diameter. Preheat the oven to 180°C/Fan 160°C/Gas 4.

STEP 1 Lightly whisk the egg and caster sugar together in a bowl. Add the mascarpone and whisk again until smooth and there are no lumps.

STEP 2 Arrange the brioche slices as neatly as possible in a single layer on the greased dish to completely cover it. Trim the brioche slices as necessary to fit. Spread the mascarpone mixture over the brioche slices to about 1cm (½ in) away from the edge. (You don't have to be accurate about this!)

STEP 3 Arrange the apricot halves neatly in circles over the mascarpone right to the edge of the brioche, cut-side down. Sprinkle the Demerara sugar over the apricots.

STEP 4 Bake in the preheated oven for about 30–35 minutes until the custard is set and golden. Dust with icing sugar, and serve immediately with crème fraîche.

AGA Bake on the floor of the Roasting Oven for about 8 minutes then slide on to the top set of runners in the Roasting Oven for a further 12 minutes until the custard is just set and golden.

PREPARING AHEAD Step 1 can be made and kept in the fridge up to 12 hours before. The brioche can be arranged in the dish, covered tightly for up to 12 hours ahead. The apricots can be drained. Assemble up to 2 hours before serving. Or bake the day before, and reheat in the oven preheated to 190°C/Fan 170°C/Gas 5 for about 10 minutes. (It is best cooked just before serving, though.)

TIP Most good supermarkets sell brioche loaves now. As you use only half the loaf, freeze the other half for another occasion.

ORANGE PANNA COTTA

Literally translated, 'panna cotta' means 'cooked cream'. It should be barely set, and it is delicious served with a sharp fruit or fruity coulis. If you prefer to make vanilla-flavoured ones, replace the orange rind with 1 teaspoon vanilla extract. As an alternative, the panna cotta can be made in a 1.2 litre (2 pint) glass serving dish. A good accompaniment to an orange panna cotta is a sliced orange fruit salad.

1 orange
2 tablespoons cold water
1 × 11g (¼ oz) packet
  powdered gelatine
900ml (1½ pints) single cream
75g (3 oz) caster sugar
finely grated rind of 1 orange

You will need 8 pretty glasses or ramekins.

STEP 1 Remove a little orange zest and save for garnishing later. Finely grate the remainder.

STEP 2 Measure the cold water into a small container and sprinkle the gelatine over evenly. Set aside to sponge.

STEP 3 Put the cream, sugar and finely grated orange rind into a saucepan and bring to scalding point (just below boiling), stirring to dissolve the sugar. Remove from the heat, and cool very slightly.

STEP 4 Add the sponged gelatine and whisk until dissolved and smooth. Pour into the glasses or ramekins and when cold, cover with clingfilm and allow to set in the fridge for about 6 hours or, ideally, overnight. If you prefer not to eat the orange rind, strain first.

STEP 5 Garnish with the reserved orange zest and serve.

PREPARING AHEAD The panna cotta can be made up to 2 days ahead, if kept in the fridge.

TIP If you prefer, you can use leaf gelatine or vegetarian gelatine. The latter is based on seaweed, the setting agent being agar-agar. If you wish to turn out individual panna cotta, use small metal pudding basins. Lightly oil the insides, and leave upside down on kitchen paper to allow excess oil to drain out. Make as above. Just before serving, gently using your index finger, pull the pannacotta from the side of the mould and turn out.

DIVINE WHITE CHOCOLATE CHEESECAKE

Serve very thin slices as this cheesecake is very rich but so delicious!

BASE
50g (2 oz) butter
150g (5 oz) plain chocolate
   digestive biscuits, crushed

FILLING
300g (10 oz) good-quality
   white chocolate
400g (14 oz) full-fat cream cheese
2 eggs
150ml (¼ pint) soured cream
1 teaspoon vanilla extract

TO SERVE
a dusting of cocoa powder
about 225g (8 oz) fresh
   raspberries

Preheat the oven to 160ºC/Fan 140ºC/Gas 3. Grease and line the base of a 20cm (8 in) deep springform cake tin with non-stick paper.

STEP 1 Melt the butter in a small saucepan over a low heat. Stir in the crushed biscuits and press evenly over the base of the prepared tin. Chill in the fridge.

STEP 2 Break the white chocolate into a bowl and melt over a pan of hot water (do not allow the chocolate to become too hot), stirring occasionally with a spoon until runny and smooth.

STEP 3 Whisk the cream cheese and eggs together in a large bowl or with the electric mixer until smooth, then add the soured cream and vanilla and whisk again until completely smooth with no lumps. Stir in the melted chocolate and mix together. Pour this mixture into the tin and spread evenly over the chilled base.

STEP 4 Bake in the preheated oven for about 45 minutes until firm around the edge and just set in the middle. Remove from the oven. Run a small palette knife around the edge of the tin, then allow to cool. Chill.

STEP 5 Remove the outside ring and lift the base on to a serving plate. Serve dusted with cocoa powder and with a few fresh strawberries or raspberries.

AGA Bake on the grid shelf on the floor of the Roasting Oven with the cold plain shelf on the second set of runners for about 15 minutes until beginning to set around the edges. Transfer the hot plain shelf to the Simmering Oven, sit the cheesecake on top and bake for about another 30 minutes until firm around the edge and just set in the middle. Remove from the oven and continue with the end of step 4.

PREPARING AHEAD You can make this the night before, and it freezes well, wrapped, after step 4.

TIP White chocolate can be tricky to use when melted, so do not allow it to get too hot, otherwise it becomes grainy. Milky Bar does not melt well – we prefer to use Lindt Continental White chocolate or Green and Black's. To avoid a really deep crack on the surface of the baked cheesecake, loosen the tin around the edge before it becomes cold.

HAZELNUT MERINGUE ROULADE WITH PASSION-LEMON COULIS

A meringue roulade with the wonderful addition of hazelnuts.
The coulis is stunning!

5 egg whites
275g (10 oz) caster sugar
50g (2 oz) shelled hazelnuts,
    roughly chopped
300ml (½ pint) double
    cream, whipped

COULIS
6 tablespoons lemon curd
2 passionfruit

GARNISH
8 Cape gooseberries

Preheat the oven to 200ºC/Fan 180ºC/Gas 6. Line a 33 × 23cm (13 × 9 in) Swiss roll tin with greased non-stick baking paper, pushing it into the corners.

STEP 1 Whisk the egg whites in an electric mixer on full speed until very stiff. Gradually add the sugar, 1 teaspoon at a time, and still at high speed, whisk well between each addition. Whisk until very, very stiff and all the sugar has been included. Mix in two-thirds of the hazelnuts.

STEP 2 Spread the meringue mixture into the prepared tin and sprinkle the remaining hazelnuts evenly over the top. Bake in the preheated oven for about 12 minutes or until just coloured pale golden. Lower the oven temperature to 160ºC/Fan 140ºC/Gas 3, and continue baking for a further 20 minutes until firm to the touch.

STEP 3 Remove the meringue from the oven and turn, hazelnut-side down, on to a sheet of non-stick baking paper. Remove the paper from the base of the cooked meringue and allow to cool for about 10 minutes.

STEP 4 When cooled, spread the whipped cream over the meringue. Start to roll from the short end, very tightly at first, until rolled up like a Swiss roll. Wrap in non-stick paper and chill before serving.

STEP 5 To make the coulis, mix the lemon curd with the scooped-out seeds and juice from the passionfruit.

STEP 6 Serve the coulis alongside a slice of roulade. Garnish with the Cape gooseberries.

AGA Cook the meringue on the grid shelf on the floor of the Roasting Oven with the cold plain shelf on the second set of runners for 8–10 minutes until pale golden brown. Transfer to the Simmering Oven for about 15 minutes until firm to the touch.

PREPARING AHEAD The roulade can be made 24 hours before it is needed. Complete to the end of step 4 and keep in the fridge. The coulis can also be made up to 24 hours ahead (this time will also allow the passionfruit seeds to soften slightly). You can also freeze the roulade: wrap in foil at the end of step 4 and freeze for up to 2 months.

TIP You can make lemon curd with the egg yolks left over from the meringue.

BRANDY ICE CREAM

This ice cream does not need a second whisking, so is very quick and easy. It is very good with mince pies and tarts – and delicious with the classic Christmas pudding instead of brandy butter. It contains raw egg yolks, so is not suitable for pregnant ladies or the very young or elderly.

4 eggs, separated
100g (4 oz) caster sugar
300ml (½ pint) double cream
4 tablespoons brandy

STEP 1 Whisk the egg whites on fast speed, using an electric hand whisk, until light and stiff. Beat in the sugar, still on a fast speed, a little at a time until you have a thick glossy meringue. Fold in the egg yolks.

STEP 2 Whisk the cream and brandy together until thick. Fold into the meringue mixture.

STEP 3 Freeze in a flat polythene box overnight, for at least 12 hours.

PREPARING AHEAD
Freeze for up to 1month.

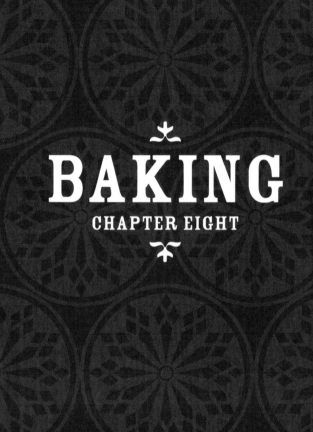

BAKING

CHAPTER EIGHT

As most of you will know, baking is one of my passions, and particularly so at Christmas time. I love creating new cakes and traybakes, and I have included here a brand-new Christmas cake recipe, along with its traditional marzipan or almond paste, and royal icing. Take care not to overbake Christmas fruitcakes as the fruit burns easily, so have some foil handy to cover the top loosely to prevent this and if cooking too fast, lower the temperature as well. But if you prefer something lighter, you can choose the American Light Christmas Cake or – although not so traditional – the Whole Orange Spice Cake or the Apricot and Brandy Cake. I have included an indulgent chocolate log cake, which will be loved by the young. If you baked only one or two of these, you would be well supplied with teatime treats for the inevitable visitors at this time of year. If there are children at home, they'll love to make the Stained Glass Window Biscuits, which would look beautiful on the tree and are also delicious to eat. And don't forget that one of the major advantages of home baking, particularly when preparing for Christmas, is that most cakes and biscuits freeze well. After they have cooled, wrap them well and freeze them un-iced for up to a couple of months.

CHRISTMAS CAKE BITES

This recipe was thought up by Lucy, my assistant. Quick to prepare and easy to share – make in a traybake, cut into squares and it is perfect for a small tea or as a canapé.

175g (6 oz) apricots, chopped
3 tablespoons brandy
175g (6 oz) butter, softened
175g (6 oz) light brown sugar
4 eggs, beaten
175g (6 oz) plain flour
225g (8 oz) raisins
225g (8 oz) currants
225g (8 oz) cherries, quartered, washed and dried

TO FINISH AND DECORATE
a little apricot jam, warmed
500g (1 lb 2 oz) packet ready-prepared almond paste (Golden Marzipan)
500g (1 lb 2 oz) packet ready-to-roll white icing

Preheat the oven to 160ºC/Fan 140º/Gas 3. Grease and line a 30 × 20cm (12 × 8 in) traybake tin with non-stick baking paper.

STEP 1 Measure the apricots into a small bowl, pour over the brandy and leave to soak overnight or until all of the brandy is absorbed.

STEP 2 Cream the butter and sugar together using an electric hand whisk until smooth. Add the remaining ingredients and mix well. Spoon the mixture into the prepared tin and level the top.

STEP 3 Bake for 1–1¼ hours until golden brown. Insert a skewer to test – if it comes out clean the cake is cooked. Set aside to cool.

STEP 4 Brush the top of the cake with apricot jam and then roll out a rectangle of marzipan the same size as the top of the cake. Lay this on top of the cake, and then brush the marzipan with a little more jam. Roll out a rectangle of icing the same size as the cake, and then cover the marzipan with the icing.

STEP 5 Slice into squares and serve with a cup of tea.

AGA Bake on the lowest set of runners in the Roasting Oven, with the cold sheet on the second set of runners for about 10 minutes. Transfer to the Simmering Oven for 2 hours or until a skewer comes out clean.

PREPARING AHEAD The cake can be made, covered and iced up to 2 days ahead. The cake also freezes well without marzipan or icing.

TIP You can cut the squares as small as you like. If you are serving this as a sweet canapé, try cutting into 50.

CLASSIC VICTORIAN CHRISTMAS CAKE

Remember to allow 3 days for marinating the fruit in sherry. This is essential to plump up and flavour the fruit. If you cut the soaking time, there will be surplus liquid which will alter the texture of the cake. (If you don't want to use alcohol, you could use the same quantity of orange juice.) You should make this cake at least 3 weeks ahead of Christmas, for if eaten too early it is crumbly. Decorate as you wish with ribbon, animals or stars. This is not a very deep cake.

175g (6 oz) raisins
350g (12 oz) glacé cherries, rinsed, thoroughly dried and quartered
500g (1 lb 2 oz) currants
350g (12 oz) sultanas
150ml (¼ pint) sherry, plus extra for feeding
finely grated zest of 2 oranges
250g (9 oz) butter, softened
250g (9 oz) light muscovado sugar
4 eggs
1 tablespoon black treacle
75g (3 oz) blanched almonds, chopped
75g (3 oz) self-raising flour
175g (6 oz) plain flour
1½ teaspoons mixed spice

TO FINISH AND DECORATE
about 3 tablespoons apricot jam, sieved and warmed
icing sugar
1 recipe almond paste (see page 202)
1 recipe royal icing (see page 202)

Grease and line a 23cm (9 in) deep round tin with a double layer of greased greaseproof paper. Preheat the oven to 140°C/Fan 120°C/Gas 1.

STEP 1 Put all the dried fruit in a container, pour over the sherry and stir in the orange zest. Cover with a lid, and leave to soak for 3 days, stirring daily.

STEP 2 Measure the butter, sugar, eggs, treacle and almonds into a very large bowl and beat well. Add the flours and mixed spice and mix thoroughly until blended. Stir in the soaked fruit. Spoon into the prepared cake tin and level the surface.

STEP 3 Bake in the centre of the preheated oven for 4–4½ hours or until the cake feels firm to the touch and is a rich golden brown. Check after 2 hours, and, if the cake is a perfect colour, cover with foil. A skewer inserted into the centre of the cake should come out clean. Leave the cake to cool in the tin.

Recipe continued overleaf

Recipe continued

STEP 4 When cool, pierce the cake at intervals with a fine skewer and feed with a little extra sherry. Wrap the completely cold cake in a double layer of greaseproof paper and again in foil and store in a cool place for up to 3 months, feeding at intervals with more sherry. (Don't remove the lining paper when storing as this helps to keep the cake moist.)

STEP 5 To decorate with almond paste and royal icing, see page 203.

AGA I always cook my Christmas cake in the Aga, mixing it a day ahead, then baking it the next day. I put it in the Simmering Oven first thing in the morning, then watch it during the day. Cook on the grid shelf on the floor of the Simmering Oven for 5–15 hours. Simmering Ovens do vary a great deal, hence the time difference. If your Aga is old and the Simmering Oven exceedingly cool, start the cake off in the Roasting Oven on the grid shelf on the floor with the cold plain shelf above on the second set of runners. Allow to become pale golden, then carefully transfer to the Simmering Oven to bake until a skewer comes out clean when inserted in the centre.

PREPARING AHEAD Prepare the fruit and soak in sherry 3 days ahead. Make the cake and wrap as in step 4. Store in a cool place for up to 3 months, following step 4. You could also freeze the cake before decorating, for up to 3 months; defrost at room temperature.

TIP Instead of covering with almond paste and royal icing, you could simply brush sieved warmed apricot jam over the top of the cake, then arrange glacé fruits and nuts over the jam. Brush again with jam.

ALMOND PASTE

In the past, marzipan was a cooked mixture, but now it is uncooked and so is the same as almond paste.

250g (9 oz) ground almonds
150g (5 oz) caster sugar
150g (5 oz) icing sugar, sifted
1 egg
1 teaspoon almond essence

STEP 1 Mix the ground almonds and sugars together in a bowl. Add the egg and almond essence. Knead with your hands in the bowl to form a stiff paste, but take care not to over-knead as this will make the paste oily.

STEP 2 Wrap in clingfilm and store in the fridge until required.

PREPARING AHEAD Prepare up to a week ahead, wrap in clingfilm and keep in the fridge. It also freezes well in a sealed polythene bag for up to a month.

TIP You can buy ready-prepared almond paste (marzipan) but it's nicest to make your own. It is not so easy to manage as bought, but has a superior flavour.

✦ COVERS A 23CM (9 IN) CAKE ✦

ROYAL ICING

Glycerine prevents the icing from setting rock hard. You can find it in small bottles in the baking section of good chemists.

3 egg whites
675g (1½ lb) icing sugar, sifted
3 teaspoons lemon juice
1½ teaspoons glycerine

STEP 1 Whisk the egg whites in a large bowl until they become frothy. Mix in the sifted icing sugar a tablespoonful at a time. You can do this with a hand-held electric whisk but keep the speed low.

STEP 2 Stir in the lemon juice and glycerine and beat the icing until it is very stiff and white and stands up in peaks.

STEP 3 Cover the surface of the icing tightly with clingfilm and keep in a cool place until needed.

PREPARING AHEAD Make up to 2 days before. Place in a bowl, cover tightly and keep in a cool place.

COVERING CHRISTMAS CAKE WITH ALMOND PASTE

☀ Do this up to 3 weeks ahead. If you are pressed for time, the almond paste can be left to dry overnight rather than for a few days, as long as you are using the royal icing for snow peaks and not flat-icing the cake. The reason for this is that the 'snow-peaked' royal icing is thick enough for the oil from the almond paste not to come through. There are two ways of putting the almond paste over the cake. The first is the quickest and gives rounded edges. The second – for which you roll a separate circle and sides from the almond paste – gives sharp edges, and this is the best to use for flat royal icing.

☀ Stand the cake upside down, flat-side uppermost, on a cake board which is 5cm (2 in) larger than the size of the cake.

☀ Brush the sides and the top of the cake with the warm apricot jam.

QUICK ALMOND PASTING

☀ Liberally dust a work surface with icing sugar then roll out the almond paste to about 5cm (2 in) larger than the surface of the cake. Keep moving the almond paste as you roll, checking that it is not sticking to the work surface. Dust the work surface with more icing sugar as necessary.

☀ Carefully lift the almond paste over the cake using a rolling pin. Gently level and smooth the top of the paste with the rolling pin, then ease the almond paste down the sides of the cake, smoothing it at the same time. If you are careful, you should be able to cover the cake with no excess almond paste to trim but, if necessary, neatly trim excess almond paste from the base of the cake with a small sharp knife. Cover the cake loosely with baking parchment and leave for a few days to dry out before icing.

ALMOND PASTING FOR FLAT ROYAL ICING

☀ Liberally dust a work surface with icing sugar, then roll out one-third of the almond paste to a circle slightly larger than the top of the cake. Use the cake tin as a guide to cut the almond paste to the exact size. Lift the almond paste on to the cake and smooth over gently with a rolling pin. Neaten the edges.

☀ Cut a piece of string the height of the cake plus the circle of almond paste on top of the cake, and another to fit around the cake. Roll out the remaining almond paste and, using the string as a guide, cut to size. Brush a little more apricot jam on the top edge of the strip as a seal, then roll up the strip loosely, place one end against the side of the cake and unroll to cover the sides completely. Use a small palette knife to smooth over the sides and joins of the paste. Cover the cake loosely with baking parchment and leave for a few days to dry out before icing.

ICING CHRISTMAS CAKE WITH ROYAL ICING

☀ Spread the royal icing evenly over the top and sides of the cake with a palette knife. For a snow-peak effect, use a smaller palette knife to rough up the icing. For smooth, flat icing, add slightly less icing sugar to the royal icing until just the consistency to gently run over the cake with the aid of a palette knife.

☀ Leave the cake loosely covered overnight for the icing to harden a little, then wrap or store in an airtight container in a cool place until needed.

Decorate with ribbon, Christmas figures or anything that your family likes.

TIP This can be done up to 2 weeks ahead. See also the introduction to putting the almond paste on the cake.

AMERICAN LIGHT CHRISTMAS CAKE

This is a lighter version of the classic Christmas cake. It is very, very important to drain and dry the pineapple well. If it is wet, the cake may become mouldy. If you would like to decorate this cake with almond paste and royal icing, do not decorate with almonds and cherries before baking.

350g (12 oz) glacé cherries
1 × 200g (7 oz) can pineapple pieces in natural juice
350g (12 oz) no-soak dried apricots
100g (4 oz) whole blanched almonds, chopped
finely grated rind of 2 lemons
350g (12 oz) sultanas
250g (9 oz) self-raising flour
250g (9 oz) caster sugar
250g (9 oz) butter, softened
75g (3 oz) ground almonds
5 eggs

TO DECORATE
whole blanched almonds
glacé cherries, halved

TO FINISH (OPTIONAL)
100g (4 oz) icing sugar, sifted

Preheat the oven to 160°C/Fan 140°C/Gas 3. Grease a 23cm (9 in) deep round cake tin, and line the base and sides with a double layer of greased greaseproof paper.

STEP 1 Cut each cherry into quarters, rinse and drain well. Drain and roughly chop the pineapple, then dry both the cherries and pineapple very thoroughly on absorbent kitchen paper. Snip the apricots into raisin-sized pieces.

STEP 2 Place the prepared fruit and nuts in a large mixing bowl with the grated lemon rind and sultanas and gently mix. Add the remaining ingredients and beat well for 1 minute until smooth. Turn the mixture into the prepared cake tin. Level the surface and decorate the top with blanched whole almonds and halved glacé cherries.

STEP 3 Bake in the preheated oven for about 2¼ hours until golden brown. Insert a skewer to test – if it comes out clean, the cake is cooked. It may be necessary after 1 hour to cover it loosely in foil to prevent it getting too brown.

STEP 4 Leave to cool in the tin for about 30 minutes, then turn out and cool completely on a wire rack.

STEP 5 You can glaze the cake if liked. Mix the sifted icing sugar with enough water to give a thin icing, and drizzle over the top of the cake.

AGA Stand a grill rack in its lowest position in the large roasting tin, and place the cake on top. Slide the roasting tin on to the lowest set of runners in the Roasting Oven, with the cold plain shelf above on the second set of runners. Bake the cake for about 30 minutes until a pale golden brown – watch very carefully. Transfer the roasting tin and cake to the Simmering Oven and cook for about a further 2½ hours until a skewer comes out clean when inserted into the cake.

PREPARING AHEAD Ideally, this cake should be made 1 month ahead and kept in the larder, covered with foil. This freezes well for up to 2 months. Thaw at room temperature for 12 hours.

MINCEMEAT LOAF CAKES

These are great to have on hand at Christmas time. They freeze superbly and make a nice present. This is one of my most popular recipes. You'll often see these on farmers' market cake stalls – it's a recipe I invented yonks ago. The mincemeat adds spice and moisture to the cakes.

150g (5 oz) soft butter
150g (5 oz) light muscovado sugar
2 eggs
225g (8 oz) self-raising flour
225g (8 oz) mincemeat
100g (4 oz) currants
100g (4 oz) sultanas
50g (2 oz) blanched almonds

Preheat the oven to 160°C/Fan 140°C/Gas 3. Grease two 450g (1 lb) loaf tins (top measurement 17 × 11cm/6½ × 4 in) and line with baking parchment.

STEP 1 Measure all of the ingredients, except for the almonds, into a large bowl and beat well until thoroughly blended. Turn into the prepared loaf tins and level out evenly. Arrange the almonds on top of each cake mixture.

STEP 2 Bake in the preheated oven for about 1¼ hours or until the cakes are golden brown, firm to the touch and a skewer inserted into the centre comes out clean.

STEP 3 Allow the cakes to cool in the tins for a few minutes, then loosen the sides with a small palette knife, turn out on to a wire rack and leave to cool.

AGA Put the tins on the grill rack in the lowest position in the large roasting tin. Bake in the Roasting Oven on the lowest set of runners with the cold plain shelf 2 sets of runners above for about 25 minutes until golden brown. Transfer the roasting tin and loaf tins to the middle of the Simmering Oven for about 35 minutes or until the cakes are golden, firm to the touch and an inserted skewer comes out clean.

PREPARING AHEAD The cakes will keep for up to 1 week. Wrap tightly in clingfilm and store in an airtight container. Or wrap the cakes and freeze for up to 2 months.

TIP Making 2 loaf cakes at one time means you have one for now and one to freeze – often a life-saver when friends arrive without warning.

APRICOT AND BRANDY CAKE

A beautifully moist, rich cake: ice it for Christmas, or serve plain at any time of year. Make the cake at least two weeks ahead so that it is not crumbly. You can feed it with more brandy once it is cooked. Turn the cake upside down and spoon over a few tablespoons of brandy. Decorate with almond paste and royal icing (see pages 202 –3).

225g (8 oz) ready-to-eat dried apricots, chopped into raisin-sized pieces
90ml (3½ fl oz) brandy
225g (8 oz) butter, at room temperature
225g (8 oz) light muscovado sugar
225g (8 oz) plain flour
5 eggs
225g (8 oz) currants
450g (1 lb) sultanas
350g (12 oz) glacé cherries, rinsed, dried and quartered

TO DECORATE
apricot jam for glaze
ready-to-eat dried apricots and glacé fruits

STEP 1 Soak the chopped apricots in the brandy overnight.

Preheat the oven to 140ºC/Fan 120ºC/Gas 1. Grease and line a 20cm (8 in) deep round cake tin with a double layer of greased greaseproof paper.

STEP 2 Cream the butter and sugar together in a very large mixing bowl, then add the remaining ingredients and continue to mix until well blended.

STEP 3 Spoon the mixture into the prepared tin and spread out evenly with the back of a spoon.

STEP 4 Bake in the preheated oven for 4–4½ hours or until the cake is a pale golden colour, feels firm to the touch and a skewer inserted into the centre comes out clean. Check after 2 hours, and if the cake is a perfect colour, cover with foil. Leave the cake to cool in the tin.

STEP 5 Turn out the cake. Glaze with apricot jam. Slice whole apricots in half horizontally and cut any large glacé fruits into slivers if rather thick. Arrange in groups over the top of the cake and glaze again.

AGA Cook on the grid shelf on the floor of the Simmering Oven for 5–15 hours. Simmering Ovens do vary a great deal, hence the time difference. If your Aga is old and the Simmering Oven exceedingly cool, start the cake off in the Roasting Oven on the grid shelf on the floor with the cold plain shelf above on the second set of runners. Allow to become pale golden, then carefully transfer to the Simmering Oven until a skewer comes out clean when inserted in the centre.

PREPARING AHEAD This cake keeps well as it is so moist. Bake, then cool completely, wrap in the lining paper and foil, and store in a cool place for up to 3 months. To freeze, wrap the cake in clingfilm, put into a large freezer bag and freeze for up to 3 months. To thaw, remove the wrappings and thaw for about 8 hours at roomtemperature.

TIP We've also tried this in a 23cm (9 in) round cake tin. It makes a shallower cake, taking about 3¾–4¼ hours' cooking time.

WHOLE ORANGE SPICE CAKE

A fresh, spiced orange cake. I used paper stars as stencils when dusting with icing sugar to give a pretty pattern, you could also use a doiley. If liked, you can ice the cake as well as fill it. Use just under half the orange filling to sandwich the cakes together, and spread the rest on top.

1 small thin-skinned orange
275g (10 oz) self-raising flour
3 level teaspoons baking powder
275g (10 oz) caster sugar
225g (8 oz) butter, softened
4 eggs
1 teaspoon ground cinnamon
1 teaspoon mixed spice

ORANGE FILLING
50g (2 oz) butter, softened
175g (6 oz) icing sugar, sifted,
   plus a little extra for dusting
2 level tablespoons orange pulp,
   reserved from the cake

Preheat the oven to 180°C/Fan 160°C/Gas 4. Grease and base-line two deep 20cm (8 in) tins with greased greaseproof paper.

STEP 1 Place the whole orange in a small saucepan, cover with boiling water and simmer until soft, about 20 minutes. Set aside to cool.

STEP 2 When the orange is soft and cold, cut in half and remove any pips. Process the whole orange, including the skin, until medium chunky. Reserve 2 level tablespoons of the orange pulp for the icing, and put the rest back in the processor. Add the remaining cake ingredients and blend until smooth. Avoid overmixing. Divide the mixture evenly between the two tins.

STEP 3 Bake in the preheated oven for 25–30 minutes.

STEP 4 Leave to cool in the tins for a few moments, then turn out, peel off the paper and finish cooling on a wire rack.

STEP 5 To make the orange filling, cream the soft butter, then add the sifted icing sugar and reserved orange pulp. Sandwich the cakes together with the icing, and sift icing sugar over the top of the cake.

AGA Bake on the grid shelf on the floor of the Roasting Oven with the cold plain shelf on the second set of runners for 20–25 minutes, turning after 15 minutes. When the cakes are cooked, they should be shrinking away from the sides of the tins and be pale golden brown.

PREPARING AHEAD Best eaten freshly made but it will store in an airtight container for 2–3 days. You could also freeze the filled cake for up to 2 months. Thaw for 2–3 hours at room temperature.

TIP Thin-skinned oranges are usually smaller – avoid using Jaffa oranges as they have a very thick pith.

TREACLE SPICE TRAYBAKE

Don't be too worried if the traybake dips in the centre – it means you were a little generous with the treacle.

225g (8 oz) butter, softened
175g (6 oz) caster sugar
225g (8 oz) black treacle
300g (11 oz) self-raising flour
2 teaspoons baking powder
1 teaspoon ground mixed spice
1 teaspoon ground allspice
4 eggs
4 tablespoons milk
3 bulbs stem ginger from a jar, finely chopped

ICING
75g (3 oz) icing sugar, sifted
about 2 tablespoons stem ginger syrup from the jar
2 bulbs stem ginger, finely chopped

Preheat the oven to 180ºC/Fan 160ºC/Gas 4. Line a small roasting tin about 30 × 23cm (12 × 9 in) with foil and grease well.

STEP 1 Measure all the ingredients for the cake into a large bowl and beat well for about 2 minutes until well blended. Pour into the prepared tin.

STEP 2 Bake in the preheated oven for about 40 minutes. Remove from the oven and allow to cool a little. Lift cake in foil case out of the tin to cool completely.

STEP 3 To make the icing, mix together the icing sugar and syrup. Pour over the cake while still warm, and sprinkle with the chopped stem ginger. If preferred, dust with sifted icing sugar.

AGA Hang on the lowest set of runners of the Roasting Oven with the cold plain shelf on the second set of runners and cook for 20–25 minutes until deep brown and set round the edges. Transfer the hot plain shelf to the centre of the Simmering Oven and slide the roasting tin on top of it. Allow to cook for 15–20 minutes until ready.

PREPARING AHEAD Make up to 2 days ahead, and ice on the day. If you want to freeze, leave whole, un-iced, wrap in foil and freeze for up to 2 months. Thaw for about 6 hours at room temperature, then ice and cut into 15–20 squares.

TIP A great standby for Christmas: it's good to give to carol singers with mulled wine.

THE ULTIMATE CHOCOLATE ROULADE

In the past I have always covered the baked roulade with a damp tea towel and left it overnight. Now I find there is no need to do this.

175g (6 oz) plain chocolate
175g (6 oz) caster sugar
6 eggs, separated
2 tablespoons cocoa
    powder, sifted

TO FINISH
300ml (½ pint) double cream
icing sugar

Preheat the oven to 180°C/Fan 160°C/Gas 4. Lightly grease a 33 × 23cm (13 × 9 in) Swiss roll tin, and line with non-stick baking parchment, pushing it into the corners.

STEP 1 Break the chocolate into small pieces into a bowl and stand the bowl over a pan of hot water; the bowl must not touch the water or the chocolate may overheat. Place the pan over a low heat until the chocolate has melted. Allow to cool.

STEP 2 Measure the sugar and egg yolks into a large bowl and whisk with an electric whisk on a high speed until light and creamy. Add the cooled chocolate and stir until evenly blended.

STEP 3 In a separate bowl, whisk the egg whites until stiff but not dry. Stir a large spoonful of the egg whites into the chocolate mixture. Mix gently, fold in the remaining egg white and the sifted cocoa powder. Spread evenly in the prepared tin. Bake in the preheated oven for about 20 minutes until firm.

STEP 4 Remove the cake from the oven, leave in the tin, cover with a dry tea towel, and leave until cold.

STEP 5 Whip the cream until it just holds its shape and dust a large piece of greaseproof paper with sifted icing sugar. Turn out the roulade and peel off the paper. Spread with the cream. Score a mark 2.5cm (1 in) in along the short edge, then roll up very tightly like a Swiss roll, using the paper to help. Do not worry when the roulade cracks – a good one should! Dust with more sifted icing sugar to serve.

AGA Place on the grid shelf on the floor of the Roasting Oven with the cold plain shelf on the second set of runners. Bake for about 20 minutes, turning after 12 minutes.

PREPARING AHEAD Complete the roulade but without the final dusting of icing sugar, cover and either keep in the fridge for 24 hours, or you could freeze for up to 1 month.

CHRISTMAS CHOCOLATE LOG

An easy Yule log, with a delicious filling and icing. The apricot jam helps the icing to stick to the cake, and is delicious too. You don't need to wait until Christmas, though: the cake can be made at any time of the year for a special occasion.

CHOCOLATE SPONGE
4 large eggs
100g (4 oz) caster sugar
65g (2½ oz) self-raising flour
40g (1½ oz) cocoa powder

CHOCOLATE ICING AND TOPPING
2 x 200g (7 oz) bars Bournville
   chocolate, in small pieces
600ml (1 pint) double cream
4 tablespoons apricot jam
icing sugar for dusting

Preheat the oven to 200°C/Fan 180°C/Gas 6. Lightly grease a 33 × 23cm (13 × 9 in) Swiss roll tin, and line with non-stick paper or baking parchment, pushing it into the corners.

STEP 1 For the sponge, whisk the eggs and sugar using an electric hand whisk in a large bowl until the mixture is pale in colour, light and frothy. Sift the flour and cocoa powder into the bowl and carefully cut and fold together, using a metal spoon, until all the cocoa and flour are incorporated into the egg mixture. (Be careful not to beat any of the air out of the mixture.)

STEP 2 Pour into the lined tin and spread evenly out into the corners. Bake in the middle of the preheated oven for 8–10 minutes until evenly brown and the sides are shrinking away from the edge of the tin.

STEP 3 Place a piece of baking parchment bigger than the Swiss roll on the work surface. Invert the cake on to the paper and remove the bottom lining piece of paper.

STEP 4 Trim the edges of the cake with a sharp knife and make a score mark 2.5cm (1 in) in along the longer edge. Roll up (from the longer edge) using the paper, rolling with the paper inside. Set aside to cool.

STEP 5 While the cake is cooling, make the icing. Melt the chocolate and 450ml (16 fl oz) of the cream in a bowl over a pan of simmering water until completely melted (be careful not to overheat; the bowl must not touch the water). Put into the fridge to cool and firm up (this icing needs to be very thick for piping). Whip the remaining cream.

Recipe continued overleaf

Recipe continued

STEP 6 Uncurl the cold Swiss roll and remove the paper. Spread a third of the icing over the surface, then spread the whipped cream on top, and re-roll tightly. Cut a quarter of the cake off from one end on the diagonal. Transfer the large piece of cake to a serving plate and angle the cut end to the side of the large cake to make a branch. Cover the surface of the cake with the melted apricot jam.

STEP 7 Put the remaining chocolate icing into a piping bag fitted with a star nozzle. Pipe long thick lines along the cake, covering the cake completely so it looks like the bark of a tree. Cover each end with icing or, if you wish to see the cream, leave un-iced.

STEP 8 Dust with icing sugar and garnish with fresh holly to serve.

AGA Cook the cake on the grid shelf on the floor of the Roasting Oven for 8–10 minutes or until shrinking away from the sides of the tin. You may need to slide in the cold plain shelf on the second set of runners if getting too brown. Follow the rest of the recipe as above. Make the icing by breaking the chocolate into a large bowl with 450ml (16 fl oz) of the cream and putting into the Simmering Oven for about 20 minutes or until melted, stirring occasionally. Then allow it to cool until thick.

PREPARING AHEAD Make completely, filled and iced, up to 2 days ahead. If there is time, though, it is best made on the day of serving. It freezes well filled, iced or un-iced for up to 1 month. Ideally it should be frozen filled and rolled but un-iced, then iced once defrosted, which ensures the icing keeps a nice shine. Defrost in the fridge overnight to serve.

STAINED GLASS WINDOW BISCUITS

These look so pretty and are great as gifts or to hang on the Christmas tree. Make holes with a cocktail skewer before baking if you want to thread ribbon and hang them.

175g (6 oz) butter, softened
100g (4 oz) caster sugar
225g (8 oz) plain flour
about 20 boiled sweets
    (different colours)

Preheat the oven to 160ºC/ Fan 140ºC/Gas 3. Line two baking sheets with non-stick paper. You will need a large star or other Christmas cutters.

STEP 1 Measure the butter and sugar into a bowl and, using a wooden spoon or spatula, beat until smooth. Add the flour and bring the dough together using your hands.

STEP 2 Roll out on a lightly floured work surface using a rolling pin until the dough is about 0.5cm (¼ in) thick. Use your large cutter to cut out the shapes. If you have a small version of your chosen cutter use this, otherwise cut the middle out of each shape by hand, leaving about 1cm (½ in) of biscuit around the edge. Arrange on the baking sheets.

STEP 3 Separate the sweets into their colours and put them in plastic bags (one colour in each bag). Crush using a rolling pin until fine grains and then sprinkle these grains in the middle of each biscuit.

STEP 4 Bake for about 12–15 minutes or until pale golden and the sweets have melted. Leave to stand on the trays for about 5 minutes. Transfer to a cooling rack and leave to cool and firm up.

AGA Bake on the floor of the Roasting Oven for 10–12 minutes.

PREPARING AHEAD Can be made up to 2 days ahead and kept in a sealed box. The biscuits freeze well.

TIP You can stick to one colour per biscuit or create a rainbow effect by mixing the colours.

ICED CHRISTMAS BISCUITS

These are lovely to make with the family – children love cutting them out and icing them too. I use white icing and silver balls but you could add food colouring for variety or to make other decorations. They look lovely as a bundle wrapped in cellophane and a ribbon to be given as gifts or hung with ribbon on the Christmas tree. You can use any cutters – try animal shapes, stars, Christmas trees etc.

100g (4 oz) butter, softened
225g (8 oz) self-raising flour
finely grated zest of 1 lemon
100g (4 oz) caster sugar
1 large egg, beaten
1 tablespoon milk
silver balls for decoration

LEMON ICING
175g (6 oz) icing sugar
about 2 tablespoons lemon juice

Preheat the oven to 190°C/Fan 170°C/Gas 5. Grease and line two baking trays with non-stick baking paper.

STEP 1 Measure the butter and flour into a bowl and rub together using your fingertips until the mixture looks like breadcrumbs. Add the lemon zest, caster sugar, egg and milk. Bring the dough together using your hands and chill for about 30 minutes.

STEP 2 Roll out thinly on a floured work surface and cut out shapes of your choice using pastry cutters. Place on the prepared baking trays.

STEP 3 Bake for 10–15 minutes until pale golden brown and firm in the middle. Carefully transfer to a wire rack to cool.

STEP 4 Sieve the icing sugar into a bowl and stir in the lemon juice until of a spreading consistency. Pipe the icing on to the biscuits or spoon on top and spread to the edges. Finish with silver balls or decoration of your choice.

AGA Bake on the grid shelf on the floor of the Roasting Oven for about 10 minutes.

PREPARING AHEAD Can be made and iced up to 2 days ahead and kept in a sealed container. They freeze well cooked – it's best to ice them after freezing and defrosting – and will keep for up to 3 months.

TIP They will firm up once out of the oven and cooling so don't be tempted to overcook them if you think they are a bit soft in the oven.

BUFFETS AND BOXING DAY

CHAPTER NINE

Meat and game dishes, particularly casseroles and stews, are perfect at Christmas time because they can be made well in advance and frozen (and they are great for serving numbers). It is a good feeling to know you have at least a couple of meals 'taken care of', which means you can concentrate your energies more on the Christmas Day lunch itself. Christmas and New Year are a time for parties in general, and several of the recipes here are perfect – the Glazed Apple Gammon, for instance, could be part of a cold buffet table, and the Spicy Mexican Lamb or the Loch RannochVenison or Game Casserole could be served as the main course of a hot buffet. I love giving parties at Christmas time. I have the whole family, of course, on Christmas Day itself, but I like to have friends and neighbours in for drinks at some point (when I would serve canapés, see pages 17–33). I might do that on Christmas Eve or Boxing Day, but then I might also give a much larger party, particularly on New Year's Eve. I love cooking for crowds, although it does require a great deal of planning, early shopping and much cooking in advance. I take enormous pleasure in hosting a party, and, with all the preparing ahead, it means you have more time to chat and drink with your friends! The majority of the recipes here are for eight to ten people but they can easily be doubled (or trebled) to serve more if you are organising a really big party. Remember, though, that if you have more guests than you have chairs, you will have to serve foods capable of being eaten with a fork only.

To save you time and last-minute work, most of the recipes here can be prepared or cooked some time in advance. Be careful, though, to cool bulk-cooked food quickly before putting in the fridge: to speed cooling up, decant a stew, say, from the hot pan into two cold dishes, cool, then chill. Thereafter you can serve whatever it is at the correct temperature: chilled, at room temperature, or well reheated in the oven or on the hob.

WHOLE ROAST FILLET OF BEEF WITH THYME

Cold rare roast fillet of beef is sheer luxury for a buffet over Christmas. So often a beautifully cooked fillet is carved too early, arranged on a platter and in an hour or so after exposing the cut surface to the air the meat turns grey – so disappointing. A very easy solution is to carve the cold fillet up to 6 hours ahead then reassemble it into a roast fillet shape and to wrap it tightly in clingfilm. Then just arrange it on the platter immediately before serving.

1.5kg (3 lb) fillet of beef, cut from the centre of the fillet
12 large sprigs of fresh thyme
3 garlic cloves, crushed
3 tablespoons olive oil
salt and freshly ground black pepper

HORSERADISH SAUCE
generous ½ × 185g (6½ oz) jar horseradish cream
3 tablespoons whipped or thick double cream

STEP 1 First marinate the beef for 24 hours. Put the fillet into a strong polythene bag with the thyme, garlic, oil and pepper. Massage the flavours into the beef for a few moments. Keep in the fridge in the marinade for up to 24 hours.

Preheat the oven to 220°C/Fan 200°C/Gas 7.

STEP 2 Heat a non-stick frying pan until hot. Lift the thyme out of the marinade and put to one side. Seal the beef on all sides using the oil from the marinade in the hot frying pan. When gloriously brown lift out on to foil in a roasting tin and sprinkle with salt.

STEP 3 Roast in the preheated oven for 30 minutes (10 minutes per 450g/1 lb). If the fillet is thin, roast for 25 minutes only. The internal temperature should be 60°C for rare if you use a meat thermometer. (Not quite so rare, 62°–63°C.) Leave to become completely cold.

STEP 4 For the horseradish sauce, mix the horseradish cream from a jar and cream together. Season with a little salt and pepper. Serve the sauce with the cold beef.

AGA Brown the marinated meat first as in step 2 on the Boiling Plate, then cook in the middle of the Roasting Oven for 20–30 minutes.

PREPARING AHEAD Marinate the fillet for 24 hours, then cook it and leave it whole up to 24 hours ahead. Chill, and take out of the fridge before carving. Carve the cold beef fillet up to 6 hours ahead, reassemble it into a roast fillet shape and wrap tightly in clingfilm. Arrange on the platter immediately before serving.

TIP Ask the butcher to tie the joint neatly so that it keeps its round shape during roasting. The centre cut is thick and gives complete round slices. This amount of beef will feed 8–12 people depending upon whether you are serving other cold meats as well.

BEEF AND SPINACH FLORENTINE

Wonderful all-in-one dish good for serving numbers.

1 tablespoon olive oil
2 onions, chopped
900g (2 lb) minced beef
2 garlic cloves, crushed
4 tablespoons flour
2 x 400g (14 oz) cans chopped tomatoes
2 tablespoons sun-dried tomato paste
250g (9 oz) chestnut mushrooms, halved
dash of sugar
450g (1 lb) fresh baby spinach
175g (6 oz) full-fat cream cheese
175g (6 oz) strong Cheddar, grated
2 eggs, beaten
salt and freshly ground black pepper
6 large sheets filo pastry
a little melted butter

Preheat the oven to 200°C/180° Fan/Gas 6. You will need a 2.5 litre (4½ pint) wide-based ovenproof dish.

STEP 1 Heat the oil in a deep frying pan or casserole and cook the onions for a few minutes. Add the mince and brown all over. Add the garlic and fry gently, and then stir in the flour. Tip in the chopped tomatoes, paste, mushrooms and sugar, and stir together well. Cover with a lid, bring up to the boil and cook for a couple of minutes. Lower the heat and simmer for about an hour on the hob until tender. Spoon into the dish and leave to become cold.

STEP 2 Meanwhile, wilt the spinach in a frying pan and then drain in a colander, squeezing out all of the water. Roughly chop the spinach and add to a bowl with the cheeses and egg. Combine well and season. Spoon the spinach on top of the beef mixture and spread out evenly.

STEP 3 Bush the sheets of filo pastry with butter and carefully place two layers on top of the spinach. Slice the remaining sheets into three, scrunch them up and arrange on top of the pastry.

STEP 4 Bake for 30–35 minutes until golden on top and bubbling at the edges.

STEP 5 Serve piping hot with a dressed green salad.

AGA Cook the mince in the Simmering Oven for about an hour. Bake on the second set of runners for 30 minutes until golden.

PREPARING AHEAD The mince can be made and placed in the dish up to 2 days ahead. The pastry can be added up to 8 hours ahead. Freezes well with the filo topping uncooked for up to 3 months.

TIP If you have home-grown spinach which you have frozen, remove the woody stem and chop the spinach, defrost and then wilt. Drain all the excess water really well.

STEAK AND KIDNEY PIE WITH PORT AND PICKLED WALNUTS

There is plenty of gravy, so keep some back from the pie and serve it separately. This does take time to make but it is marvellous to make completely ahead. It's great for a family gathering.

about 2 tablespoons sunflower oil

1.5kg (3¼ lb) skirt beef, or good stewing steak, cut into 4cm (1½ in) cubes

500g (1 lb 2 oz) ox kidney, trimmed and cut into 4cm (1½ in) pieces

2 large onions, roughly chopped

75g (3 oz) butter

75g (3 oz) plain flour

900ml (1½ pints) beef stock

150ml (¼ pint) port

2–3 tablespoons Worcestershire sauce

2 tablespoons redcurrant jelly

salt and freshly ground black pepper

250g (9 oz) button mushrooms, left whole

1 × 390g (14 oz) jar pickled walnuts, drained and walnuts halved

500g (1 lb 2 oz) puff pastry

1 egg, beaten

You will need a pie dish with a lip, of about 33 × 26 × 6cm (13 × 10½ × 2½ in), with a capacity of 2.2 litres (4 pints). When ready to cook the whole pie, which is possibly a day after you have started, preheat the oven to 220°C/Fan 200°C/Gas 7.

STEP 1 Heat a little oil in a casserole and fry the beef and kidney cubes until brown all over (you may need to do this in batches). Lift out on to a plate using a slotted spoon, and set aside.

STEP 2 Heat a little more oil in the unwashed casserole, add the onion and fry for a few minutes over a high heat. Stir in the butter and melt, then blend in the flour, followed by the beef stock and port. Blend well, stirring all the time, until thickened, then add the Worcestershire sauce and redcurrant jelly.

STEP 3 Return the meat to the casserole and season with salt and pepper. Bring up to the boil, cover and simmer for about 3 hours or until the beef is tender.

STEP 4 Half an hour before the meat is ready, stir in the mushrooms and pickled walnuts. Taste for seasoning, then arrange the meat in the pie dish. Pour over most of the gravy so the dish is filled nearly up to the top, and reserve the remaining gravy to serve separately. Place an inverted handle-less cup or pie funnel in the centre of the dish (with the meat all around).

Recipe continued overleaf

Recipe continued

STEP 5 Set aside to cool in the fridge overnight or as long as possible so the filling sets.

STEP 6 Roll out the pastry on a lightly floured surface to the same shape as the dish but about 5cm (2 in) wider all the way round. Cut strips from around the pastry about 2.5cm (1 in) wide to use on top of the lip of the pie dish. Wet the lip of the dish, lay the thin strips of pastry on top, and brush with beaten egg. Carefully lift the rolled pastry on top of the dish and push down the edges so they stick to the pastry on the lip. Trim off any excess pastry and flute the edges. Glaze with beaten egg. Cut out shapes from the pastry trimmings, and use to decorate the top, glazing these with egg as well.

STEP 7 Bake in the centre of the preheated oven for 30–40 minutes, turning around halfway through, cooking until the meat bubbles. If the pastry is getting too brown, cover loosely with foil.

STEP 8 Serve with the remaining gravy, heated through, thinning it down with water if necessary.

AGA Bring the steak and kidney to the boil on the Boiling Plate. Put the lid on, and transfer to the Simmering Oven until tender, about 3 hours. Cool as above and continue with step 6. Bake the pie on the lowest set of runners in the Roasting Oven for 30–40 minutes, turning around halfway through, until the meat is piping hot and the pastry is golden brown.

PREPARING AHEAD Keep in the fridge unbaked for up to 24 hours. The pie freezes well with the raw pastry topping (for up to 2 months), before cooking in the oven. Thaw before cooking.

TIP If you don't like pickled walnuts, just leave them out.

FILLET STEAK WITH WILD MUSHROOM SAUCE

All prepared ahead and reheated. It's a foolproof way of cooking fillet steaks. Serve with a delicious mushroom sauce.

4 × 175g (6 oz) thick beef
   fillet steaks, cut from
   the centre of the fillet
olive oil
salt and freshly ground
   black pepper
a little butter

WILD MUSHROOM SAUCE
25g (1 oz) butter
1 garlic clove, crushed
2 level tablespoons plain flour
scant 75ml (2½ fl oz) Madeira
1 × 400g (14 fl oz) can beef
   consommé
175g (6 oz) mixed wild
   mushrooms (chestnut,
   oyster and shiitake), sliced
2 generous tablespoons
   crème fraîche
1 tablespoon chopped
   fresh parsley

Preheat a ridged grill pan over a high heat until very hot.

STEP 1 Oil the steaks lightly on both sides, and season well. Sear the steaks on the grill pan for 2 minutes on each side for medium rare; a little longer if you like the steaks well done. Rest for 10 minutes while you make the sauce. Place on a baking sheet. When cold, place in the fridge covered with clingfilm. Preheat the oven to 220ºC/Fan 200ºC/Gas 7.

STEP 2 To make the sauce, melt the butter, and add the garlic. Blend in the flour, off the heat, followed by the Madeira and consommé. Add the sliced mushrooms. Return to the heat, and bring to the boil, stirring until thickened. Add the crème fraîche and parsley, and check the seasoning.

STEP 3 To reheat, bring the steaks to room temperature 30 minutes before you want to continue cooking. Uncover them, and smear the smallest amount of butter on top of each. Place in the preheated oven for 7 minutes. Don't leave them longer, otherwise they will be overcooked. Reheat very thin steaks for 6 minutes.

STEP 4 Reheat the sauce in a pan on the hob and serve with the steaks.

AGA Sear on the Boiling Plate in a ridged pan. To reheat, cook on the second set of runners in the Roasting Oven for about 7 minutes.

PREPARING AHEAD For the steaks, complete steps 1 and 2, up to 12 hours ahead. The sauce can be made the day before and kept in the fridge.

GAME CASSEROLE

Vary the proportion of meats as you like, and, if you have difficulty getting the exact amounts of mixed game, you can make up the difference with braising beef or boneless chicken. In season, some supermarkets sell packs of mixed game – often including venison, pheasant, rabbit, wild duck and pigeon.

1.4kg (3 lb) mixed game meats (see above)
2 tablespoons sunflower oil
75g (3 oz) butter
200g (7 oz) smoked bacon lardons
450g (1 lb) whole frozen chestnuts, thawed
4 leeks, thickly sliced on the diagonal
50g (2 oz) plain flour
300ml (½ pint) red wine
600ml (1 pint) chicken stock
4 tablespoons redcurrant jelly
salt and freshly ground black pepper
1 large orange

TO SERVE
2 tablespoons chopped fresh parsley
1 orange, sliced

STEP 1 Trim the meats and cut into 5cm (2 in) pieces.

STEP 2 Heat the oil and half of the butter in a large non-stick frying pan or casserole, and brown the game and bacon over a high heat until sealed and brown. You will have to do this in batches. Add a little more oil if necessary. (Don't be tempted to put too much meat in the pan at once as it won't seal or brown properly.) Remove with a slotted spoon and set aside.

STEP 3 Add the remaining butter to the frying pan and brown the chestnuts. Lift out with a slotted spoon and set aside. Add the leeks to the pan and fry over a high heat for a few minutes.

STEP 4 Sprinkle in the flour, and gradually blend in the red wine, stock and redcurrant jelly. Bring to the boil, stirring, season with salt and pepper, then add the whole orange and the meats.

STEP 5 Cover and cook over a low heat for 1½–2¼ hours or until the meats are tender. You could also cook the casserole in the oven preheated to 160°C/Fan 140°C/Gas 3 for about the same time. (The cooking time will depend on the variety of meats used: venison, for example, tends to take a little longer to become really tender.) Check the liquid halfway through cooking, adding a little more stock if necessary.

STEP 6 About 15 minutes before the end of the cooking time, add the whole chestnuts.

Recipe continued overleaf

Recipe continued

STEP 7 Once the game is tender, lift the softened orange into a sieve, cut in half, stand over a bowl and push the orange through the sieve, collecting the juice. Gradually stir the juice into the casserole until the taste is perfect. Check the seasoning and add some more stock if the casserole is still a little thick.

STEP 8 Garnish with freshly chopped parsley and orange slices. Serve with mashed potato and fresh vegetables – Celeriac Purée and Braised Red Cabbage (see pages 135 and 136) go particularly well.

AGA Cook as above up to the end of step 4 on the Simmering Plate. Bring to the boil on the Boiling Plate, cover and transfer to the Simmering Oven for about 2½ hours until tender. Continue as above.

PREPARING AHEAD Casseroles are often even better a day or so after cooking as the flavours have a chance to mellow, and this one is no exception. Cook the casserole as directed. Cool quickly, cover and keep in the fridge for up to 2 days. Reheat gently until piping hot, adding a little more liquid if needed. To freeze, prepare the casserole to the end of step 7, cool quickly and freeze for up to 3 months. Thaw thoroughly, then reheat gently until piping hot, adding more liquid if necessary. Garnish with chopped parsley and orange slices.

TIP To serve as individual pies, cook the casserole as directed. Roll out a 375g (13 oz) packet of ready-rolled puff pastry so that it is a little larger and cut out eight 10cm (4 in) circles. Crimp the edges of each circle and lightly mark a diagonal pattern on the surface. Glaze with beaten egg and bake at 200°C/Fan 180°C/Gas 6 for about 15 minutes until golden brown (this can be done ahead). Serve a spoonful of casserole on a plate and slant a puff pastry circle on top to make a 'pie'.

HIGHLAND PHEASANT CASSEROLE WITH APPLES

If you haven't game stock, use chicken stock cubes. For a special occasion, prepare a few more apple wedges and fry in butter. Serve alongside the pheasant as a garnish. This is wonderful served with mash.

25g (1 oz) butter
2 tablespoons sunflower oil
salt and freshly ground
    black pepper
6 pheasant breasts, skinned
2 onions, thinly sliced
25g (1 oz) plain flour
150ml (¼ pint) apple juice
300ml (½ pint) game stock
2 dessert apples, peeled
    and cut into thin wedges
2 tablespoons double cream
1 tablespoon lemon juice

STEP 1 Heat half the butter and all the oil in a large non-stick frying pan until very hot.

STEP 2 Season the pheasant breasts, and brown them in the hot frying pan over a high heat until brown, 1–2 minutes on each side. Set aside.

STEP 3 Heat the remaining butter in the unwashed frying pan, add the onions and fry until it is tender and its wetness has evaporated, 10–15 minutes.

STEP 4 Sprinkle in the flour and gradually blend in the apple juice and stock. Bring to the boil, stirring, then add the apples and pheasant breasts, and season with salt and pepper. Cover and simmer over a low heat for about 12 minutes or until the pheasant breasts are just cooked through. Do not overcook.

STEP 5 Stir in the double cream and lemon juice, check the seasoning and serve hot.

AGA Bring to the boil after seasoning in step 4, cover and transfer to the Simmering Oven for about 15 minutes until the breasts are just cooked.

PREPARING AHEAD Cook a day ahead to the end of step 4, slightly undercooking, then reheat gently, adding the cream and lemon juice. You can also freeze it at the end of step 4, for up to a month. Defrost and reheat, adding the cream and lemon juice.

TIP Pheasant legs are not suitable for this recipe as the cooking time is very short, and legs need long, slow cooking otherwise they are tough.

GLAZED APPLE GAMMON

Ham is always a top favourite, whether served hot or cold. When you cook a ham at Christmas time, use the skin placed over the turkey breast as an excellent way to keep the breast moist while roasting. Gammon is a raw cured bacon leg cut, and it is called ham when it is cooked. For a change we have cooked this one in apple juice which complements the meat perfectly (use the sort you buy in cartons).

4kg (9 lb) half gammon, unsmoked
2 litres (3½ pints) apple juice
2 generous tablespoons redcurrant jelly
1 tablespoon Dijon mustard

STEP 1 Place the gammon in a large pan just big enough to hold it, and cover with the apple juice. Bring to the boil over a high heat. Turn the heat down to simmer, cover and cook very gently for about 4 hours (55 minutes per kg, 25 minutes per lb) until tender. I advise using a meat thermometer (the thermometer should read 75°C when done), but put it in at the end as it must not be submerged in liquid. To test for doneness without a thermometer, pierce the gammon with a skewer – it should feel tender as the skewer goes into the meat.

STEP 2 Allow the meat to cool in the liquid. Remove from the pan, and place on a piece of foil in a small roasting tin. Gently remove the skin, leaving the fat on top. Melt the redcurrant jelly, stir in the mustard and spread evenly over the fat of the ham. Score the glaze diagonally with a sharp knife, cutting through the fat. Wrap the lean meat in foil.

STEP 3 Glaze and brown under the grill or glaze in a preheated oven at 220°C/Fan 200°C/Gas 7 until golden brown and crisp – about 15 minutes.

STEP 4 If serving cold, chill in the fridge for 12 hours or so before carving.

AGA Bring to the boil on the Boiling Plate, cover and transfer to the Simmering Oven for about 4–5 hours (depending on your Simmering Oven) until tender. Glaze at step 3 in a roasting tin on the highest set of runners in the Roasting Oven until golden brown and crisp.

PREPARING AHEAD
The completed gammon can be made up to 6 days ahead and kept in the fridge.

TIP Check with your butcher when you buy your gammon whether or not it needs to be soaked before cooking to remove the saltiness. Supermarket gammon usually does not need soaking as the cure is milder.

MEXICAN SPICY LAMB

A warming casserole, perfect for buffets over Christmas. Serve with salad and garlic bread. If you have difficulty getting black-eyed beans, use red kidney beans instead.

900g (2 lb) neck fillet of lamb, trimmed of any fat
2 tablespoons sunflower oil
2 garlic cloves, crushed
1 large onion, sliced
2 level tablespoons plain flour
1 teaspoon ground cumin
1 teaspoon ground coriander
150ml (¼ pint) white wine
1 × 400g (14 oz) can chopped tomatoes
2 level tablespoons tomato purée
salt and freshly ground black pepper
2 × 400g (14 oz) cans black-eyed beans, drained and rinsed
2 generous tablespoons mango chutney

TO SERVE
1 × 150g (5 fl oz) tub Greek yoghurt
sprigs of fresh coriander or mint

Preheat the oven to 160°C/Fan 140°C/Gas 3.

STEP 1 Cut the lamb into 5cm (2 in) cubes. Heat half the oil in a large pan, add the lamb and brown in batches over a high heat. Remove the lamb with a slotted spoon on to a plate, and set aside.

STEP 2 Lower the heat, and add the remaining oil and the garlic and onion to the pan. Allow to soften for a few minutes, then blend in the flour and spices, and allow to cook for a further 2 minutes.

STEP 3 Add the wine, tomatoes and tomato purée then add the browned meat. Bring to the boil, season with salt and pepper, cover and transfer to the oven for about 2 hours, until the meat is tender.

STEP 4 Stir in the beans and chutney, and cook for a further 10 minutes.

STEP 5 Serve with Greek yoghurt seasoned and mixed with 2 teaspoons chopped coriander or mint if liked.

AGA Sear the lamb on the Boiling Plate. Cook the onion on the Boiling Plate. At step 3, cook, covered, in the Simmering Oven for 1½–2 hours or until the meat is tender.

PREPARING AHEAD Prepare to the end of step 3. Cool, cover and keep in the fridge for up to 2 days. Or freeze at the end of step 3, for up to 3 months. In both cases, add the beans and chutney when reheating.

LOCH RANNOCH VENISON

A wonderful rich winter casserole which is perfect for entertaining.
Serve it with redcurrant or other fruit jelly, or serve simply with
mashed potato for the family.

900g (2 lb) stewing venison,
   cut into 2.5cm (1 in) pieces
25g (1 oz) butter
100g (4 oz) smoked streaky bacon,
   snipped into small pieces
350g (12 oz) whole shallots
   or small pickling onions
2–3 garlic cloves, crushed
50g (2 oz) plain flour
300ml (½ pint) red wine
600ml (1 pint) chicken stock
1 tablespoon tomato purée
1 tablespoon runny honey
1 head celery, cut diagonally
   (reserve the heart for later)
225g (8 oz) chestnut mushrooms,
   whole or, if large, halved
salt and freshly ground
   black pepper
celery leaves or fresh parsley

Preheat the oven to 160ºC/Fan 140ºC/Gas 3.

STEP 1 Brown the venison in the butter in a frying pan
over a high heat. Spoon into a large casserole.

STEP 2 Cook the bacon in the same frying pan until the fat
begins to run. Add the whole shallots and the crushed garlic,
and fry for 4–5 minutes. Add the flour, stir well, then blend
in the wine and stock. Add the tomato purée, honey, celery
(not the heart), mushrooms and seasoning. Bring to the boil,
and simmer for 5 minutes. Pour the sauce over the venison
in the casserole.

STEP 3 Cover the casserole, and transfer to the preheated
oven for 2 hours, or until tender. Add the chopped celery
heart for the last 20 minutes of the cooking time. This
adds crunch to the casserole.

STEP 4 Check the seasoning, skim off any fat, and garnish
with celery leaves or parsley.

AGA After step 2, cover and
transfer to the Simmering
Oven for 1½–2½ hours.

PREPARING AHEAD After step 3,
quickly cool, cover and chill for
2 days. You could also cool the
casserole, pack it and freeze,
at the end of step 3, for up to
3 months.

WATERCROFT CHICKEN

If you are looking for something really special to serve over the holiday period, this is a winner.

6 chicken breasts,
    boneless, skin on
salt and freshly ground
    black pepper
2 tablespoons lime marmalade
25g (1 oz) butter

MUSHROOM FARCE
50g (2 oz) butter
3 shallots, finely chopped
350g (12 oz) button mushrooms,
    coarsely chopped
50g (2 oz) breadcrumbs
    (about 2 slices)
1 small egg, beaten

SAUCE
150ml (½ pint) good chicken stock
juice of 1 lime
1 × 200ml (7 fl oz) carton full-fat
    crème fraîche
lots of chopped fresh parsley

Preheat the oven to 200ºC/Fan 180ºC/Gas 6.

STEP 1 For the mushroom farce, melt the butter in a pan and sauté the shallots for about 1 minute. Lower the heat and cook gently for about 10 minutes. Add the mushrooms, and toss quickly in the butter over a high heat. Remove from the heat, add the breadcrumbs and a little egg (you may not need it all), and season well. Leave to cool.

STEP 2 To stuff the chicken breasts, pull back the skin at one side, leaving it attached at the other side. Season and stuff under the skin, then fold back. Put all the chicken pieces in a large greased roasting tin.

STEP 3 Put the marmalade into a saucepan with the butter, and heat very gently, stirring well, until the marmalade has melted and combined with the butter. Brush the chicken pieces with this mixture.

STEP 4 Roast in the preheated oven for 15–20 minutes until golden brown. Remove from the oven, transfer the chicken to a warmed serving dish using a slotted spoon, and keep hot while you make the sauce.

STEP 5 To make the sauce, scrape all the bits from the base and sides of the roasting tin, add the stock and stir briskly over the heat to reduce a little. Add the lime juice and crème fraîche and heat gently, stirring well, until it has a smooth creamy consistency. Season, add the chopped parsley and serve with the chicken.

AGA Roast on the top set of runners in the Roasting Oven for about 15 minutes.

PREPARING AHEAD Make the stuffing ahead of time and cool. Stuff the chicken, cover and refrigerate for up to 24 hours. You could also freeze the raw, stuffed chicken for up to 3 months.

TIP This is for Aga cooks only. Chicken breasts, quail or rack of lamb roast quickly but the steam can prevent browning, so I glaze them with something such as redcurrant jelly which gives the meat both colour and gloss. Here I use marmalade – which also, of course, adds flavour!

CLARET CHICKEN WITH THYME AND CRISPY BACON

The great advantage of this recipe is that the sauce can be made well ahead, then just spooned over the marinated chicken breasts.

6 small chicken breasts, boneless and skinless
2 tablespoons brandy
2 fat garlic cloves, crushed
225g (8 oz) streaky bacon, cut into strips (or buy ready-cut lardons)
1 large onion, sliced
250g (9 oz) chestnut mushrooms, sliced
1 tablespoon sunflower oil
25g (1 oz) butter
50g (2 oz) plain flour
300ml (½ pint) red wine
300ml (½ pint) chicken stock
1 tablespoon each of tomato purée, soy sauce and redcurrant jelly
salt and freshly ground black pepper
1 tablespoon chopped fresh thyme
2 tablespoons chopped fresh parsley

Preheat the oven to 200ºC/Fan 180ºC/Gas 6.

STEP 1 Put the chicken breasts into a polythene bag and add the brandy and crushed garlic. Seal the top of the bag and massage the flavours into the chicken for a minute. Leave to marinate for as long as possible in the fridge; overnight is ideal.

STEP 2 Fry the bacon over a high heat until crisp, remove with a slotted spoon, drain on kitchen paper and set to one side.

STEP 3 Add the onion to any bacon fat in the pan, cook for 2–3 minutes over a high heat, then lower the heat, cover and cook for about 20 minutes until soft.

STEP 4 Remove the lid, turn up the heat, add the mushrooms and fry for 2–3 minutes, adding the oil and butter. Lower the heat, stir in the flour and slowly blend in the red wine and stock, stirring all the time. Bring to the boil, add the tomato purée, soy sauce, redcurrant jelly, seasoning and thyme, and boil for a few minutes.

STEP 5 Arrange the chicken breasts in an ovenproof dish in a single layer. Pour the sauce over the chicken, cover with foil and cook in the preheated oven for 20–30 minutes until the chicken is tender. The timing depends on the size of the chicken breasts and temperature of the sauce. Reheat the lardons, uncovered, in the oven for about 10 minutes.

STEP 6 Sprinkle the lardons and parsley over the chicken to serve.

AGA Cook on the second set of runners in the Roasting Oven for about 20 minutes (see step 5).

PREPARING AHEAD Sauces (without cream) and gravies can be made up to 2 days ahead and kept in the fridge, or they can be frozen. The lardons can be made ahead and stored in the fridge.

TIP If time really is short, forget marinating the chicken, and add the garlic and brandy to the sauce. Fresh thyme is easy to grow in the garden or in a window box outside.

GLAZED ORIENTAL DUCK WITH PAK CHOI

Duck breasts with a wonderful flavoured sauce, which may be made well ahead. If you buy breasts other than Barbary – which will probably be smaller – adjust the cooking times accordingly.

6 duck breasts, skin removed
salt and freshly ground
   black pepper
a little soft butter
1 tablespoon sunflower oil
350g (12 oz) pak choi,
   sliced into 5cm (2 in) pieces
   (keep the white stalks and
   leaves separate)

SAUCE
1½ level tablespoons cornflour
100g (4 oz) dark muscovado sugar
450ml (¾ pint) pineapple juice
3 tablespoons white wine vinegar
1½ tablespoons soy sauce
1½ tablespoons hoisin sauce
1 tablespoon sunflower oil
a good 4cm (1½ in) piece fresh
   root ginger, peeled and grated
2–3 garlic cloves, crushed

AGA Sear the duck breasts on a ridged grill pan on the Boiling Plate for 1 minute on each side. Lift on to a roasting rack in the roasting tin and slide on to the grid shelf on the floor of the Roasting Oven for about 7 minutes if you like the duck pink in the centre, or 10 minutes if you like it well done. Rest the duck for 10 minutes before slicing. Make the sauce on the Simmering Plate.

STEP 1 Season the duck breasts with salt and pepper and spread with a little soft butter on one side. Heat a ridged grill pan and sear the duck breasts, butter-side down at first, for 1 minute on each side. Lower the heat and cook the duck for about a further 7 minutes if you like the duck pink in the centre, or 10 minutes if you like it well done. Rest the duck for 10 minutes before slicing.

STEP 2 To make the sauce, measure the cornflour, sugar and 6 tablespoons of the pineapple juice into a bowl and mix until smooth. Add the remainder of the pineapple juice, the vinegar, soy and hoisin sauces.

STEP 3 Heat the sauce oil in a frying pan and gently cook the ginger and garlic for a few moments. Pour in the contents of the bowl, and stir continuously as the mixture comes to the boil. Strain the sauce, check the seasoning, and add any duck juices.

STEP 4 Heat the sunflower oil in a large frying pan, add the white pak choi stalks and stir-fry over a high heat for 2–3 minutes until almost tender. Toss in the leaves and stir-fry until just wilted. Season.

STEP 5 To serve, spoon the pak choi into the centre of six hot plates. Arrange the duck slices on the pak choi and spoon the hot sauce around the outside.

PREPARING AHEAD Sear the duck up to 24 hours ahead. Cool, cover and chill in the fridge. Roast in the oven preheated to 200ºC/Fan 180ºC/Gas 6 for about 10 minutes. The sauce can also be made a couple of days ahead.

TIP Buy pineapple juice in a carton, the kind that you would buy for breakfast.

TURKEY KORMA

A very good hot way of using up the last cuts of the turkey at Christmas, but also excellent with chicken at any time of year. Ensure your turkey is still fresh off the carcass – not one that has been hanging around for days, in and out of the fridge. Serve with rice or naan bread, poppadoms and mango chutney.

450g (1 lb) cooked turkey, cut into neat pieces
150g (5 oz) green seedless grapes, cut in half lengthways
2 tablespoons chopped fresh coriander or parsley

KORMA SAUCE
1–2 tablespoons sunflower oil
3 large onions, very roughly chopped
2 fat garlic cloves, crushed
1 teaspoon ground cardamom
5cm (2 in) piece fresh root ginger, grated
1 tablespoon ground cumin
1 tablespoon ground coriander
1 tablespoon garam masala
300ml (½ pint) turkey or chicken stock
1 × 200ml (7 fl oz) carton coconut cream (UHT)
salt and freshly ground black pepper
50g (2 oz) ground almonds

STEP 1 Heat a large frying pan, add the oil and onions, and fry over a high heat for a few minutes.

STEP 2 Lower the heat, cover the pan and soften for about 20 minutes.

STEP 3 Add the garlic, cardamom, ginger, cumin, coriander and garam masala to the onions. Fry for a further few minutes over a high heat to roast the spices.

STEP 4 Stir in the stock and coconut cream, bring to simmering point, season and stir in the ground almonds to thicken.

STEP 5 Add the cooked turkey to the hot sauce, and bring back to the boil. Cover and simmer very gently over a low heat for about 10 minutes until the turkey is piping hot.

STEP 6 Stir in the grapes and sprinkle over the chopped coriander.

AGA Start the onions on the Boiling Plate, then cover and transfer to the Simmering Oven for about 30 minutes.

PREPARING AHEAD Most sauces such as korma sauce can be made well ahead and kept in the fridge for 2–3 days. They can then just be reheated and the cooked meat dropped into them and reheated for 5 minutes or so.

SPICY TURKEY FAJITAS

If using raw turkey, marinate for half an hour and fry the meat in batches with the spring onions and red pepper until golden and cooked.

about 700g (1½ lb) cooked turkey breast, cut into thin strips
juice of 2 limes
a dash of Tabasco sauce
2 tablespoons olive oil, plus a little extra
salt and freshly ground black pepper
12 wheat fajitas or tortillas
8 spring onions, finely sliced on the diagonal
1 large red pepper, thinly sliced
¾ teaspoon each of ground coriander, turmeric and paprika

TO SERVE
soured cream or crème fraîche
romaine or Cos lettuce
mango chutney

Preheat the oven to 160ºC/Fan 140ºC/Gas 3.

STEP 1 Marinate the turkey with the lime juice, Tabasco, olive oil and salt and pepper. Leave for at least 30 minutes.

STEP 2 Wrap the 12 fajitas or tortillas flat in foil and warm in the preheated oven for about 5 minutes, or in a microwave in clingfilm for about 30 seconds.

STEP 3 Heat a little oil in a frying pan and fry the spring onions and red pepper until cooked. Add the turkey to the pan with the spices and fry for a further few minutes. Pour over any remaining marinade and cook for a further minute.

STEP 4 Put the soured cream or crème fraîche, lettuce and mango chutney in three separate bowls. Transfer the warm fajitas to a basket, and spoon the meat into a serving dish.

STEP 5 To serve, everybody helps themselves. Spread half of each fajita with mango chutney, soured cream, lettuce and turkey and vegetables. Roll up and enjoy.

AGA Warm the fajitas on a plate tightly covered with clingfilm. Put into the Simmering Oven for no more than 30 minutes (or in a 4-oven Aga Warming Oven for up to 1 hour). Stir-fry the ingredients on the Boiling Plate.

PREPARING AHEAD Marinate the turkey up to 24 hours ahead.

TIP You can of course use cooked chicken in this dish instead of the turkey.

EASTERN CURRY WITH FRUITS

A great hot party dish and very easy. It's also perfect for using leftover turkey but be sure to make it while the turkey is still fresh, not a few days later. If you like a really spicy flavour, add an extra teaspoon of curry powder. We serve this hot but it could be served cold, without heating in the oven just before serving.

900g (2 lb) cooked turkey, cubed
10 spring onions
2 perfect ripe avocados, stoned, peeled and sliced
2 mangoes, stoned, peeled and sliced
4 bananas, slightly underripe, diagonally sliced
juice of 2–3 lemons, according to size
50g (2 oz) butter
2 good tablespoons medium curry powder
1 × 600g (1 lb 5 oz) jar thick low-calorie mayonnaise
1 × 360g (12 oz) jar mango chutney, large pieces cut up
salt and freshly ground black pepper
paprika

Preheat the oven to 220°C/Fan 200°C/Gas 7.

STEP 1 Chop the spring onions, keeping the white and green parts in separate piles. Toss all the fruit in the juice of the lemons. All these want to be in fairly chunky pieces.

STEP 2 Melt the butter in a saucepan and fry the white part of the spring onions until tender. Add the curry powder, allow to cook for a few minutes, then mix with the mayonnaise and the chutney in a large bowl.

STEP 3 Mix all the fruits, lemon juice, green spring onion and turkey with the mayonnaise mixture, and check the seasoning. Pile into a shallow ovenproof dish about 30 × 38cm (12 ×15 in). Sprinkle with paprika.

STEP 4 Just before serving, bake in the centre of the preheated oven for 15–20 minutes, watching carefully, until piping hot. Do not allow to overcook or the mayonnaise will separate. Serve with rice and a green salad.

AGA Fry the spring onions and curry powder on the Boiling Plate. Bake in the centre of the Roasting Oven for 12–15 minutes, watching carefully, until piping hot. Be careful not to overcook or the mayonnaise will separate.

PREPARING AHEAD Combine the turkey with the mayonnaise mixture and the green part of the spring onions up to a day ahead. Cover and keep in the fridge. Cut the avocados, mangoes and bananas just before cooking. Toss in the lemon juice and add to the mixture.

FIVE-SPICE MANGO TURKEY

This is perfect to serve cold for a buffet or when cooking for numbers, as it is so light and fresh – and there is not a drop of mayonnaise in sight! It can be made a day ahead and kept in the fridge, which gives time for the flavours to really infuse into the turkey.

750g (1¾ lb) fresh cooked turkey meat, without bone
salt and freshly ground black pepper

MANGO SAUCE
2 large mangoes, peeled
8 mild peppadew peppers from a jar
6 tablespoons mango chutney
1 × 200ml (7 fl oz) carton Greek yoghurt
1 tablespoon Chinese five-spice powder
juice of 1 lemon
a few drops of Tabasco sauce

GARNISH
fresh salad leaves
2 mild peppadew peppers, thinly sliced
lots of chopped fresh parsley

STEP 1 For the sauce, cut the flesh of one mango roughly into pieces and put in the food processor. Add the rest of the ingredients, and whiz until smooth and blended. Season with salt and pepper.

STEP 2 Cut the turkey into neat pieces and mix with the mango sauce in a mixing bowl. Cut the flesh of the remaining mango into 1cm (½ in) pieces and stir into the turkey mixture. Taste and check the seasoning.

STEP 3 Spoon the turkey mixture into a dish, garnish with a few salad leaves, and sprinkle over the peppadew slices and parsley. Serve cold.

AGA To serve hot, slide on to the second set of runners in the Roasting Oven for about 15 minutes until very hot. Sprinkle with peppadew slices and serve.

PREPARING AHEAD If you want to make this a day ahead, omit adding the chopped mango and leave it mixed with a little lemon juice in a bowl in the fridge. Just stir in before serving.

TIP To serve hot (I really was surprised this worked so well!), simply add 1 tablespoon cornflour to the mango mixture before blending in the processor. Then add the turkey and mango, pile into a shallow ovenproof dish, and bake at 200°C/Fan 180°C/Gas 6 for about 15 minutes until sauce is bubbling. Sprinkle with peppadew slices and serve.

THREE BEAN, TOMATO AND ASPARAGUS SALAD

V

This can be made ahead completely as the beans can marinate in the dressing and the tomatoes will not lose too much liquid. Serve on a stylish platter for your buffet table.

1 × 400g (14 oz) can lentils
1 × 400g (14 oz) can
   flageolet beans
1 × 400g (14 oz) can
   black-eyed beans
4 spring onions, sliced
   on the diagonal
6 tablespoons good
   salad dressing
salt and freshly ground
   black pepper
225g (8 oz) asparagus tips
10 tomatoes, skinned and sliced
1 tablespoon balsamic vinegar
   mixed with 2 tablespoons
   olive oil
a handful of freshly snipped
   chives and torn basil leaves

STEP 1 Drain and rinse the lentils and beans. Pat dry on kitchen paper, then mix together in a bowl. Stir in the spring onions, salad dressing and salt and pepper. Arrange along the base of a thin flat dish.

STEP 2 Blanch the asparagus tips in boiling salted water for 4–5 minutes until just tender, drain and refresh in cold water. Dry on kitchen paper.

STEP 3 To look very attractive arrange the tomato slices over the beans, overlapping. Arrange the asparagus tips in a herringbone shape along the centre of the tomatoes or serve as you wish.

STEP 4 Season with salt and pepper, then drizzle the balsamic vinegar and oil mixture over the whole dish. Sprinkle over the chives and basil, and serve.

PREPARING AHEAD
Make completely to the end of
step 3 up to some 12 hours ahead.

POTATO, CELERY AND CARAMELISED ONION SALAD

V

Adding the dressing to the potatoes while they are still warm helps the flavours to be thoroughly absorbed. This can also be served as a warm salad, which would be delicious with cold turkey or as part of a buffet.

1kg (2¼ lb) baby new
   potatoes, scrubbed
salt and freshly ground
   black pepper
8 celery sticks, thinly sliced
   on the diagonal
3 tablespoons olive oil
1 onion, thinly sliced

DRESSING
8 tablespoons mayonnaise
6 tablespoons light olive oil
3 tablespoons lemon juice

STEP 1 Slice the potatoes in half lengthways and cook in a pan of boiling salted water for about 15 minutes or until just tender. Drain the potatoes thoroughly, allow to cool slightly, then peel off as much skin as you can. Tip into a bowl and mix in the celery.

STEP 2 Meanwhile heat the oil in a large non-stick frying pan and cook the sliced onion for 5–10 minutes until golden brown. Move the onion slices around the pan occasionally to help them to caramelise evenly. Lift out with a slotted spoon on to kitchen paper and allow to cool.

STEP 3 Whisk the dressing ingredients together in a small bowl, seasoning to taste with salt and pepper.

STEP 4 Pour the dressing over the potatoes and celery whilst the potatoes are still warm. Mix gently. Turn into a warm serving dish and scatter the caramelised onion over the top to serve.

AGA Boil the potatoes in boiling salted water on the Boiling Plate until just tender, 10–15 minutes.

PREPARING AHEAD Prepare the salad the day before, cover and keep in the fridge.

HERBY TABBOULEH

V

Perfect for a Christmas buffet table, make sure that this is well seasoned, with the flavours of the lemon and olive oil foremost. Tabbouleh should be bright, bright green from the herbs, and you should hardly be able to see the wheat at all.

225g (8 oz) bulgar wheat
finely grated zest and juice
  of 2 lemons
6 spring onions, finely sliced
1 large bunch of fresh mint,
  roughly chopped
1 large bunch of fresh flat-leaf
  parsley, roughly chopped
2 tablespoons extra virgin
  olive oil
1 cucumber, peeled, deseeded
  and cut into 1cm (½ in) cubes
salt and freshly ground
  black pepper

STEP 1 Measure the bulgar wheat into a saucepan, and cover with water. Bring to the boil and gently boil for 10–12 minutes until soft. Drain, refresh in cold water and drain well again.

STEP 2 Tip the bulgar wheat into a bowl and mix in the remaining ingredients. Season well with salt and pepper.

PREPARING AHEAD Make the bulk of the salad a couple of hours in advance but do not add the cucumber until the last moment, otherwise it will become soft and make the salad too wet.

TIP Bulgar wheat, also known as burghul, bulgur or cracked wheat, is a product made by parboiling wheat, drying it, then coarsely grinding it. Look on the packet for cooking instructions – some wheats do not need much cooking.

INDEX

ACKNOWLEDGEMENTS

This book has been a joy to write
with a very special team.

Firstly, thank you to Lucy Young, who has so
many talents. My assistant of over 20 years, she is
creative, always there with new ideas, often a twist
on a classic making it more modern and up to date.

Lucinda McCord, who has been with us 13 years
now, diligently testing recipes to our high standards
with patience and fun.

Jo Roberts Miller, the best editor we have ever
had, this is now the fourth book we have worked
together on and Jo is a joy.

Thanks to my agent Felicity Bryan, Jonathan Taylor
and the Headline team, Smith & Gilmour the design
agency for the stunning design, Martin Poole for the
superb photography and the lovely Kim Morphew
the home economist, who is so talented.

How lucky I am to have such a lovely team.

PICTURED RIGHT
Lucinda McCord, Mary and Lucy Young

Mary Berry is well known as the author of more than seventy cookery books with total sales of over 5 million. She has presented a number of television series and is currently a judge on *The Great British Bake Off*. She contributes to radio programmes and cookery magazines, and is loved for her practical and unfussy approach. She gives many demonstrations around the country but when she is at home, she loves to be with her family and tending her garden – her other great passion.